CHOICES
AND
REWARDS

How to Live the Life
God Loves to Bless

David
CERULLO

THE
INSPIRATION
NETWORKS

D0168467

CHOICES AND REWARDS

Published by
The Inspiration Networks
P.O. Box 7750
Charlotte, NC 28241

Book design: Koechel Peterson and Associates, Inc. Mpls., MN

Printed in the United States of America

This book is dedicated to the Friends and Partners
of The Inspiration Networks.
My hope is that these words will encourage you
to make the right choices in your life…
choices God will reward in this life
AND in the life to come.

David

CONTENTS

INTRODUCTION

A S I BEGAN TO WRITE THIS BOOK, I felt the Lord impressing upon me, "David, there are three kinds of people who need this message."

First, the Lord said, "One category is those who are on the brink of making the worst choices they will ever make in their lives. They will regret the consequences of these decisions for eternity. But, if they will stop right now and listen to Me, I will help them make the right choices."

Next, He told me, "There are others reading this message who are on the verge of making some of their *greatest* and most important decisions. If they will make the choices I am setting before them, I will reward them for taking a step of faith and obedience. I will open the windows of Heaven and pour out blessings upon them that will last throughout this life—and precede them into the life to come."

Finally, He said, "There is a third group of people who are bound with fear, doubt and uncertainty—those who have vacillated from one decision to the next.

I want these people to know that unless they begin to walk by faith and not by fear, unless they step out and make the right choices, they won't receive anything from Me."

Regardless of the category in which you find yourself, I believe the Lord has placed this book into your hands for His Divine Purpose. God wants you to know that today, and every day of your life, you are making choices that affect your family, your finances, your personal and spiritual life—plus much more. As we will discover, the decisions we make today not only have a dramatic impact during our life on earth, but also for Eternity.

As much as some people would like to avoid this subject, *every* choice we make—whether good or bad—has an unavoidable reward. It's like the law of physics: *for every action there is a reaction.*

From the beginning, God established principles by which we are to live. Then He gives us a choice: we either can accept or reject His Word—obey or disobey. As sure as the sun will rise tomorrow, for each decision, there *IS* a consequence.

In these chapters, you will learn:

- How to make the most important choice of your life.
- What God says about blessings and curses.
- How decisions affect your reputation.
- How choices affect your relationships.
- Decisions that can defeat the devil.
- Ten steps to making wise choices.
- How to determine your destiny.

It is my prayer that as a result of what you are about to read, you will understand the importance of even your *smallest* choices, and gain the wisdom and knowledge necessary to make the *right* decisions—those that are in the very center of God's will.

I am thrilled we are taking this rewarding journey together.

— David Cerullo

YOUR POWER TO CHOOSE

Between two evils
choose neither;
between two goods,
choose both.

TYRONE EDWARDS

Decisions! Decisions! Decisions! We make hundreds—even thousands of them—every day.

Black sweater or blue? Coffee or tea? KFC or Taco Bell? Paper or plastic? Answer the phone or let it ring? Read my Bible now or wait until later? Drive the main road or take a shortcut? Listen to the news or pop in a CD?

Our routine choices may seem insignificant, yet all our decisions affect us in one way or another. Hidden in this constant drumbeat of decision-making are major turning points—options we take that become major chapters in our life story.

SHOULD I GRUMBLE AND COMPLAIN?

As a child, I was faced with a tough decision.

I thank the Lord that I was privileged to have a father—many don't. Yet, I grew up with mine being gone most of the time. My dad, evangelist Morris Cerullo, was called by God to preach the Gospel and build an army of ministers worldwide. As a result, he was away from home almost 300 days of the year. While other boys my age had their fathers around to watch them play baseball or football, my dad was somewhere in the four corners of the earth— Africa, Asia, South America, and beyond.

I had a choice to make. I could grumble, complain, and make life miserable for my parents, or I could willingly give my father to the nations of the world without murmuring. I chose to make that sacrifice.

In my early years, our family (I have a sister, Susan, living; and a brother, Mark, with the Lord) would journey together to Dad's crusades. When we reached school age, however, my parents made the decision that it was best for us to stay in one location and let him travel alone.

As a youngster, my father would occasionally take me with him to an overseas crusade. It was exciting to experience a foreign culture, and those trips made a lasting impression on me. I saw the humble living conditions—the huts, the starvation, and the abject poverty. I also witnessed firsthand the spiritual starvation of hearts hungry for the Gospel.

Even then, I was making decisions pertaining to my future. When I saw the power of God open blind eyes, unstop deaf ears, and cause the lame to walk, the Lord began stirring something within me. At this young age, I was developing a heart for the Lost and a special compassion for the suffering.

A DOCTOR?

I began to pray, "Lord, I want to do something to make a difference in the world."

Not once did I feel drawn to become a preacher. Instead I thought, "If I could be a medical doctor, God could use me to help alleviate sickness and pain in people's lives. "While other boys went through stages, dreaming of becoming a policeman one minute and a fireman the next, I always wanted to be a doctor.

For some reason, I constantly seemed to be in a hurry. I graduated from high school early and applied to the University of California at San Diego, which had a great medical school. I was on my way!

One small detail: As a teenager, I entered into what I thought was a serious "love interest" with a girl. We even talked marriage!

When my parents heard the news, they went ballistic! As kindly as they could, they said, "Son, you're crazy!

What are you thinking? You're far too young. You have your whole life ahead of you!" And they added, "Most importantly, we don't feel this person is right for you spiritually."

I was devastated. My parents convinced me to go to school out of state to Oral Roberts University and "try it" for one semester. If I didn't like the school, I could come home and go to the University of California at San Diego. So at 17 years of age, I enrolled in the pre-med program at ORU and began to follow my dream.

Not long afterwards, in God's Providence, I met a beautiful girl in Tulsa named Barbara, who three years later would become my wife. Suffice it to say, I wasn't going home to San Diego!

GOD'S QUESTION

Two years into my college experience while studying at my dorm room desk, God suddenly spoke to me: "David, what about My Kingdom?" Then He repeated the question. "David, what about My Kingdom?"

My response was, "What about it Lord? I'm studying medicine. I'm going to be a doctor to help heal suffering humanity."

God continued asking, "What about My Kingdom?"

It became abundantly clear that the Lord had other plans for my life. He was asking me to lay down my career in medicine and make a different *choice* about my future. For as long as I could remember, I wanted to be a physician, and now God was asking me to take another route.

I began praying, "Lord, if you want me to lay aside medicine and follow you in ministry, I will." Even then, I didn't feel God leading me to be a minister in the traditional sense. Instead, I believed I was to change my college major to business, so I did.

You see, when I was growing up, Dad never talked to me about entering the ministry—or even working with him at sometime in the future. But I truly felt that if I could help relieve the burden of the business and administration of his worldwide outreach, he could be more effective by focusing on the ministry itself. I called my father and shared my decision with him.

I asked, "Dad, do you feel there is a place for me in your ministry in San Diego?"

"Of course there is!" he replied.

Again in a hurry (why, I don't know, but I always seemed to be in a hurry!), I changed majors and graduated one year early. Barbara and I were soon married, and off to San Diego we went.

The choices I made during those early years proved pivotal in the journey God had planned for our life and family.

CHANGE YOUR CHOICES!

I am excited about your reading these pages. Why? Because I believe the message God has asked me to share with you is absolutely vital for you and those you love.

Years ago I heard these compelling words: *If you want to change your future, change your choices!*

Think about that statement for a moment. Do you realize how the decisions you make today impact everything about tomorrow? It's true! We are the sum total of our life choices—whether for good or bad.

From the moment of creation, the Almighty has given His children an awesome, life-changing power—the power to choose. He did not make us puppets with heavenly strings; rather He has given us a freewill to make moral choices. We have the responsibility to choose between God or Satan, life or death, wisdom or folly, obedience or sin.

The decisions we make not only affect our future on earth: They determine *where*—and *how*—we will spend eternity.

CHOICES BRING REWARDS

Destiny is not a matter of chance,
it is a matter of choice:
it is not a thing to be waited for,
it is a thing to be achieved.

WILLIAM JENNINGS BRYAN

Have you ever stopped to think about how the choices you make now in this life affect not only your future here on earth, but also affect your future in Eternity? Your choices bring rewards. Choices bring consequences. The choices you make today determine your future.

God asks us all to make important choices. You make choices that affect your family, your future, and the "here and now," but you also make choices that very much affect the "there and then" of Eternity.

You are the sum total of all the choices you've made in life from earliest childhood to where you are today. Where you are in life now—your job, your family, your present circumstances—are all a result of the choices you made from the decisions God set before you. Choices always have consequences for good or for bad.

God's Word is full of promises, rewards and consequences. In Leviticus 26, you'll find 40 verses of blessings and curses. The Lord said, *"If you walk in my statutes and keep my commandments and do them, **then** I will give you rain in due season. Then the land will yield its increase"* (26:3-4).

In Deuteronomy 28, there are 68 verses focusing on blessings and curses. The Lord says in His Word, *"It shall come to be, if you diligently obey the LORD your God, being careful to do all His commandments which I command you today…all these blessings will come upon you and overtake you if you obey the LORD your God"* (vv. 1 & 2).

It's interesting that the first 14 verses in Deuteronomy 28 tell of the blessings from God, but the next 53 verses speak about curses. For some reason, God uses four times as many verses in this passage of Scripture to talk about the curses He would bring upon us for making the wrong choices than He does in explaining the blessings we would receive from Him for making the right choices.

Apparently, God is more interested in our understanding the consequences of making the wrong choice than He is in our understanding the consequences of making the right choice. Why? Why does God focus so much on the consequences of our making *wrong* choices? My guess is that He wants us to think long and hard about the consequences of making wrong choices!

WHAT ABOUT TODAY?

God clearly sets before us choices and decisions to make. His Word says that if we obey Him and make the right choices, we will have a positive reward. And if we disobey Him and make the wrong choices, He curses us. It's that simple.

I know "curses" is a strong word to use, but this is what the Bible says, not me. You may be reading this book and saying, "Well, wait a minute, David. The books of Leviticus and Deuteronomy are in the *Old Testament.* That was all the *Old Covenant*—written under the law. Today, God has given us a *New Testament,* a *New Covenant.* We live under grace now."

Well, I believe this is true, but listen to what Deuteronomy 29 also says: *"Now, and not with you alone, am I making this covenant and this oath but with those who stand here with us today in the presence of the Lord our God* **and with those who are not with us here today"** *(29:14, 15).*

Also, listen to what the Apostle Paul wrote in his first letter to the Corinthians: *"But with many of them God was not well pleased for they were overthrown in the wilderness. Now these things were our examples"(10:5).* In the eleventh verse Paul says, *"All these things happened to them as an example to us."*

You know, I love grace, and I'm so thankful God renews His grace to us each and every day. But we can't keep running around as so many like to do saying, "Grace, grace, grace," and then use grace as a license to choose unwisely.

Paul asks in Romans 6:1-2: *"What shall we say then? Shall we continue in sin, that grace may abound? God forbid."* Where God's law was present in the Old Testament, there was also God's *grace*; where you find grace in the New Testament, believe me, there is still God's *law*.

THE COMING HARVEST

Let's get back to choices. My friend, the most important choice God will ever ask you to make is to accept the gift of His Son Jesus Christ and make Him the Lord of your life or to reject Him as your Lord and Savior. The consequences of *this* choice determine *where* you're going to spend Eternity. But other choices you make in life, your behavior and actions—those choices and decisions unlock the door to God's rewards, and they determine *how* you're going to spend eternity.

The choices you make about the Seeds you Sow in this lifetime—Seeds of love, prayer, gentleness, kindness, giving—these Seeds produce a bountiful Harvest of rewards, now in this lifetime, but they also produce Harvest of rewards that are waiting for you in Eternity.

Sadly, many people don't stop to think about the consequences of other kinds of Seeds they Sow—Seeds of anger, bitterness, harsh words, even gossip. These Seeds also bear Harvests of rewards, now in this lifetime AND in Eternity.

YOUR COMPENSATION

The Harvests of rewards you produce are a result of the Seeds you Sow. Jesus said in Matthew 16:27, *"The Son of Man is going to come in the glory of His Father with His angels and then He will reward each according to his works."*

When most people think about rewards, they think about good things, positive things. A reward is something special, isn't it? Well, no. That's really a misinterpretation of the word "reward." A reward is simply compensation—something received in return for something done. A reward can be good or bad.

Compensation really means to weigh one thing against another. Imagine for a moment the old-fashioned scales people used to weigh something. You would place what you wanted to weigh on one side of the scale and put a known weight on the other side. You weighed one thing against another. You were looking for an equivalent weight. Which is heavier? Which is lighter? But equivalent to what?

What's the equivalent compensation in terms of the choices you make? It's the equivalent of what you do. Jesus says your rewards will be according, or equivalent, to your works.

Now, you may not consciously go though your day making choices based on a reward you expect to receive, thinking, "Well, if I do *this* God will reward me." Yet, your right choices will bring a lifetime of rewards, now in this life AND in the life to come.

There is another side to this "coin." Wrong choices will result in a lifetime of pain, regret and sorrow—not just in this life, but also in the life to come.

THE THREE "T'S"

Here are three things God gives each of us:
- **Time**—God gives each of us 24 hours a day, seven days a week.
- **Talent**—God gives each of us different talents and gifts.
- **Treasure**—God gives each of us different treasures.

We all have the opportunity to invest what we have been given. It's *how* we choose to *Sow* our time...how we choose to *use* our talents...how we choose to *invest* the treasure He's given us that determine our rewards now in this lifetime and later in Eternity.

I keep stressing "now in this lifetime" and "later in Eternity" because I talk to so many people who just think about today. They live in, and for, the "now." But we have a life after "now," and it's a lot longer than "now," believe me!

We're finite human beings. We have no comprehension of time. Eternity is something I have a hard time understanding. But in this life, the Lord says that maybe we'll live three score and ten—that's 70 years. Or, if we're strong, maybe we'll live another ten years to age 80 (Psalm 90:10). What is 80 years compared to the scope of eternity? It's not even a vapor or a blink of an eye.

Yet many people spend so much time making choices that affect them here and now, and they forget about the choices that are going to affect them there and then.

Jesus promises in Revelation 22:12 that He's coming again and that He's bringing rewards with Him to give to each person according to their works. I Corinthians 3:8 declares, *"Each will receive his own reward according to his own labor."* Revelation 20:13 says, *"They were judged every man according to their works."* By now it should be very clear: *where* you spend Eternity depends on what you believe, but *how* you spend Eternity depends on the choices you make—here.

YOUR "WAGES"

What you do today affects not only you and your family here in this lifetime, but the consequences affect your life forever. Jesus has a lot to say about rewards. He taught in Luke 14 that we will be repaid at the resurrection of the just—that's after we have passed on from this life—for good deeds and works we've done.

He also said in Matthew that our rewards come after we're in Heaven as a result of what we did here on earth. In Luke 6:23, Jesus said, *"Rejoice in that day and leap for joy for indeed your reward is great in heaven."*

When you translate the word "reward" that Jesus used in this passage, it means "wages." So, Jesus is saying your wages—what you've worked so hard to earn—are going to be great. Your *repayment* will be in return for something you did.

Jesus used the same word in the story of the Good Samaritan in Luke 10. He said, *"I will repay you."* It's the same word He used in Mark 9:41 when He said, *"Whoever gives a cup of water in my name will by no means lose his repayment."*

I love what the writer of the book of Hebrews states: *"Without faith it's impossible to please God for he who comes to God must believe that He is and that He is a rewarder of those who diligently seek Him"* (Hebrews 11:6). Yes, God is a Rewarder.

One day soon, we're going to stand in the Presence of God, and He is going to present our "wages" for the choices and actions we took here on this earth, whether those choices had good or bad consequences.

God's Divine scales will be placed before us. Our good choices are going to be stacked up on one side—the bad choices are going to be stacked up on the other side. Which way are the scales of your life going to tip?

A MANSION?

Jesus said, *"In my Father's house are many mansions— and I go to prepare a place for you"(John 14:2).* So many people have taken for granted that they have a mansion, as the song says, "just over the hilltop—in that bright land where I'll never grow old." I'm not so sure that we all have a mansion just over the hilltop. I'm not so sure we all will have a palatial estate on the other side. The *"place for you"* may be entirely different from what you expect. I encourage you to study the Word and see what He's really saying. What you are going to be "living in" in Heaven…the rewards you're going to receive…are going to be in response to the choices you made here on this earth—what you did with your time, your talent and your treasure. It will not be the same for every person.

Pay close attention to how Paul describes what lies ahead: *"We must all appear before the judgment seat of Christ that each one may receive the things done in the body accord- ing to what he has done whether good or bad" (II Corinthians 5:10).*

He doesn't say we're going to be judged on the basis of our beliefs. When you invited Jesus Christ into your life, you made a choice on *where* you would spend Eternity. But He did say we're going to be judged and tested on the basis of our *works.* They are what determine our level of living in Heaven.

"SUFFER LOSS" IN ETERNITY?

If what you do with your life—the choices you make—endure as gold, silver and precious stones, you will be positively rewarded. If, on the other hand, your choices amount to hay, wood and stubble, guess what is going to happen? They will burn up, and there's going to be little or nothing left on that scale to reward (I Corinthians 3:12-15).

To me, the sobering point of I Corinthians 3 is simply this: *"If anyone's work is burned, he's going to suffer loss."* You may ask, "How do you suffer loss in Heaven? Is this possible? Isn't Heaven the *prize*? Isn't this the *hope*? Isn't that the *land* we're all trying to reach?"

Well, yes, but Paul makes it clear that it's possible to reach Heaven and still suffer loss. Loss of what? *Loss of the reward you might have received if only you had made the right choices.* However, because you made the wrong choices, your reward is placed on a fire and burned up.

As we continue, it's so important to keep in mind that every choice we make brings a reward—both now in this lifetime AND in the world to come.

AN EXAMPLE TO US

*People seldom improve
when they have no other model
but themselves to copy.*

OLIVER GOLDSMITH

I encourage you to go through your Bible, starting at the beginning of Genesis through to the end of Revelation. Make a list of all the choices people made in the Bible and the consequences of those choices. Some made wise choices and received great rewards. Others made foolish choices and suffered as a result.

At every turn in God's Word—in the lives of Ruth, David, Solomon, Elisha, Daniel, Jonah, and so many more— we see the result of choices. Their lives and the choices they made are examples to us. The rewards they received—the consequences of their choices—speak to us today.

Notice what the Apostle Paul writes to the Believers at Corinth. Speaking of the children of Israel, he says, *"With most of them God was not well-pleased; for they were laid low in the wilderness" (I Corinthians 10:5)*. Then he adds, *"Now these things happened to them as an example, and they were written for our instruction" (v.11)*.

The experiences of those who have gone before—their choices and rewards—and their entire lives are lessons for us today as we face our own choices and rewards.

THE FIRST CHOICE

We often forget that our very existence is the result of a choice by God Himself. He desired to have a family on earth with whom He could have fellowship—that was His reward.

When God created Adam and Eve, He gave them a perfect world in which to live, and there was only one word of caution. The Lord instructed them: *"From any tree of the garden you may eat freely; but from the tree of the knowledge of good and evil you shall not eat, for in the day that you eat from it you will surely die" (Genesis 2:16-17)*.

However, the first man and woman *chose* to disobey God. As a result, sin, sickness, and death entered the world. Even more, man lost his direct fellowship with God.

"LORD, WHAT'S RAIN?"

In Genesis 6, the Lord commanded Noah to build an ark. What was Noah's choice? To obey or to disobey.

"Noah, it's going to rain," announced the Almighty.

"Rain, Lord? What's rain?" (Until that point in time, people had never seen rain; the Bible only describes a "mist" that covered the earth.)

"Noah, you're going to need to build an ark," the Lord instructed.

"What's an ark?" he likely asked.

Can you imagine this conversation taking place between you and God? Think about all your friends gathering around to watch what you are doing!

"What are you building?" his friends asked.

"An ark," replied Noah.

"Why?" they wanted to know.

"Because God said it's going to rain!"

"What's rain? What's an ark?" they inquired. "Noah, you're crazy!" they concluded.

For 120 years, Noah built the ark—and took the embarrassment. He chose to endure the ridicule and obey God.

What was his reward? What did he receive as the consequence of his choice to obey? Not only were Noah and his family saved from the flood, but the entire world was re-populated, and through his seed would come the Savior of the world!

Notice that the first action of Noah when he left the ark was to build an altar and offer a sacrifice (Genesis

8:20). That decision produced an amazing reward. After God smelled the soothing aroma (the offering), He declared, *"I will never again curse the ground on account of man, for the intent of man's heart is evil from his youth; and I will never again destroy every living thing, as I have done" (v.21).*

As a result of Noah's obedience, *and* as a direct consequence of his offerings, God blessed him abundantly (Genesis 9:7). The Lord also established His Covenant with him (v.11).

I shudder to think what would have happened if Noah had not built an altar and offered a sacrifice. Would God have destroyed the earth with no survivors? Would He have started over here or on some other planet? Or not at all?

Today, perhaps the greatest thing we can do—both *during* a crisis and *after* one—is to *"offer the sacrifice of praise to God continually, that is, the fruit of our lips giving thanks to his name" (Hebrews 13:15 KJV).*

OBEDIENCE HAS ITS REWARDS

Are you beginning to see God's pattern? For every choice we make, there is a reward. And the reward is not always good—sometimes what we receive is an unwanted consequence.

The Lord told Abram, *"Go forth from your country, and from your relatives and from your father's house, to the land which I will show you; And I will make you a great nation, and I will bless you, and make your name great; And so you shall be a blessing; And I will bless those who bless you, and the one who curses you I will curse. And in you all the families of the earth will be blessed" (Genesis 12:1-3).*

Abram had a choice to make. He could stay where he was—or leave his home and trust God to bring His Will to pass. Abram was faced with the choice of turning his back on everything that was comfortable and familiar—his home, his friends, his surroundings and even his family. It was a huge step of faith!

Because he chose to respond to the voice of the Lord, God gave him, and his descendants, the land (Genesis 13). What would have been the consequences if Abram had not obeyed God?

The Bible makes it clear that disobedience also produces negative rewards.

DON'T BE IMPATIENT

Since Abram and Sarah had no children, Sarah grew impatient with God and said to her husband, *"Now behold, the Lord has prevented me from bearing children. Please go in to my maid; perhaps I will obtain children through her"* (Genesis 16:2).

So if the Lord *prevented* Sarah from having children, why did she send Hagar to Abram? Sarah and Abram made a foolish and unwise choice…and they suffered the consequences of that choice.

They chose to do things their own way instead of according to God's plan and the reward—or consequence—was the birth of Ishmael. Even though he was not the "son of promise" God had spoken of, his seed was multiplied. Ishmael was the son born of impatience and disobedience.

What has been the outcome of Sarah and Abram's choice? For thousands of years, there has been strife, tension and bloodshed in the Middle East as the sons of

Ishmael and the sons of Isaac have battled. The reward for Abram and Sarah's wrong choice has gone far beyond the boundaries of their own family as four thousand years later, this struggle encompasses not just Arab and Jew, but all mankind.

I agree with many Biblical scholars who believe the present conflict in the Middle East stems from Abram and Sarah's misguided choice. Ishmael's birth was not God's intention for them, nor for the world.

GREATER BLESSINGS!

Abram was 99 years old when the Lord once more appeared to him, saying, *"I am God Almighty; Walk before Me, and be blameless" (Genesis 17:1)*. Even more, God made a Covenant with him and changed his name to Abraham—the father of many nations (Genesis 17:5).

Despite their old age, God gave Abraham and Sarah a son, Isaac. The Lord established an everlasting Covenant with Isaac and with his seed after him (v.19). Still, the Lord was not finished with the testing of Abraham. God asked him to make a choice to obey Him and offer Isaac on the altar of sacrifice (Genesis 22).

You see, God had made a Covenant with Abraham to bless him and that his children would be as numerous as the stars in the sky. Yet, in the face of this Covenant Promise, God asked Abraham to offer Isaac as a sacrifice. How could God's promise possibly come true if Abraham were to offer Isaac as a sacrifice? Abraham didn't try to reason with God; instead he *chose* to believe God would somehow provide a sacrifice.

My friend, obedience is a *choice*. Because Abraham chose to obey, God intervened, saying: *"Do not stretch out your hand against the lad, and do nothing to him; for now I know that you fear God, since you have not withheld your son, your only son, from Me" (Genesis 22:12).* Instead, the Lord prepared a substitute—a ram to be slain on the altar of sacrifice.

Through this experience, God renewed His Covenant with Abraham. Earlier, the Lord said He would bless him and multiply his seed. Now God was declaring He would *greatly* bless him: *"I will greatly bless you, and I will greatly multiply your seed as the stars of the heavens and as the sand which is on the seashore; and your seed shall possess the gate of their enemies" (Genesis 22:17).*

Abraham received a *greater* reward because of his choice to obey!

TRIUMPH OR TRAVAIL?

As we are discovering, the decisions we make can have a profound impact on our personal life, family, finances and so much more—now, AND in Eternity. That's why I want you to see the "cause and effect" pattern God has established for our choices—they result either in joy or sorrow, triumph or travail.

Do you remember the story of Jacob wrestling with an angel—probably God Himself? (Genesis 33). Jacob chose not to give up, but to prevail. He would not let go until he was blessed and received the answer to his heart's cry. As a reward, God changed his name from Jacob to Israel. Instead of seeking the blessing, he *became* a blessing. Jacob's walk and his talk were transformed—God changed his entire destiny because he chose to prevail!

FEAR OR FAITH? YOU CHOOSE

Think about Moses. Here was a man hand-picked by God to deliver His people out of their bondage in Egypt. What would have happened if Moses had refused to obey?

During their great Exodus out of Egypt, the children of Israel chose to grumble and complain in the wilderness, allowing fear to rule their hearts and tongues. Growing restless while waiting for Moses to come down from the mountain of God, they made a god of their own—a golden calf. Because they chose to corrupt themselves, they reaped a reward of punishment. The Bible records that 3,000 people died that day because of their disobedience (Exodus 32:28).

Again and again, God tested the children of Israel by offering them choices. Obedience brought blessing, health, provision and victory in battle. Failure to follow God's direction resulted in punishment.

THEY SAW GRASSHOPPERS

When the 12 spies were sent to Canaan for a firsthand look at the Promised Land, 10 returned saying: *"The people whom we saw in it are men of great size...and we became like grasshoppers in our own sight, and so we were in their sight"* (Numbers 13:32-33).

Only two spies, Joshua and Caleb, reported a land filled with milk and honey, exclaiming, *"We should by all means go up and take possession of it, for we will surely overcome it"* (Numbers 13:30). They believed God would deliver the land into their hands.

Ten of the spies brought a fear-filled report. "We saw

giants in the land. There is no way we can take this country." Their fear and lack of faith struck terror into the hearts of the children of Israel.

Instead of remembering how God delivered them from the land of Egypt...

...the mighty miracles God performed with the plagues He brought against the Egyptians

...how God opened the Red Sea and swallowed Pharaoh and his army

...how God miraculously fed them in the wilderness for 40 years

...how the Almighty gave them water to drink

...how He supernaturally cared for them, not even allowing the sandals on their feet to wear out.

...instead of remembering these marvelous things, they chose to believe a negative report—to doubt God and His ability to drive out the inhabitants of the land they were told to enter.

On the threshold of the Promised Land, all 12 of the spies saw the giants, but only 10 of them viewed themselves as grasshoppers, while the other two spies saw God!

Allowing fear to rule their hearts, the people chose to believe the grasshopper report. Is it any wonder that as the consequence of their faithlessness, God allowed the children of Israel to wander aimlessly in the wilderness for 40 years until the entire generation of grumbling, complaining, faithless people died?

When you look at the circumstances you face and the choices you must make, are you like the 10 spies who were filled with fear and saw themselves as inferior grasshoppers? Or, are you like the two spies who saw God and had faith to believe that their victory was assured?

You have the right to choose to see the Lord—to

believe He will do what He says He will do—and to live by the promises of His Word!

REWARDS OF RIGHT CHOICES

Here are just a few of the consequences and rewards for choices found in the Bible for you to consider:

• When you *choose* to allow other people to tell you something different from what God has told you, bad things happen (I Kings 13).

• When you *choose* to put your faith in others instead of putting your faith in God, He says your reward...your repayment...your consequences are going to be His judgment (II Kings 1).

• When you *choose* to be unfaithful to the Lord, He will *choose* to humble you. (II Chronicles 28) You may cry out, "Lord, I thought I lived under Your grace. I thought I was under the cloud of Your forgiveness. Why am I going through this?" And God responds, "You *chose* to be unfaithful to Me, despite what My Word says."

• When you *choose* to follow a plan that is not God's, He warns: *"Woe to those who choose to execute a plan that is not the Lord's, who choose to make an alliance that is not of His Spirit, who go to the world to take refuge and safety. Your reward will be shame and humiliation"* (II Chronicles 28).

• When you *choose* to walk according to the stubbornness of your own heart and don't listen to the Lord, He will declare calamity against you. (Jeremiah 16)

HOWEVER!

• When you *choose* to be persistent with God, He will hear and answer your prayers (II Kings 4; Luke 18).

• When you *choose* to spend time in His Presence, then His peace, blessings and prosperity come (I Chronicles 13).

Do you need peace today? Do you need blessings? Do you need prosperity? Spending time in His Presence will provide you with all of these!

• When you *choose* to praise and worship God and give Him thanks in the face of your adversity, you will be rewarded with victory (II Chronicles 20). Are you facing a problem today? Do you need an answer to prayer? Praise and worship God, giving Him thanks for answering your prayer even before you see it come to pass, and see what God will do!

• When you *choose* to humble yourself before God, His Word says He will hear you (II Chronicles 34). Choose today to humble yourself before Him!

• When you *choose* to return to the Lord, He says you will find compassion, mercy, grace and forgiveness. Do you need these blessings from Him today? Then draw near to Him, and He will draw near to you! (James 4:8)

I love the verse in John 15:16 where the Lord makes it clear that He made a choice. He *chose* you and ordained that you should go and bring forth fruit, and that your fruit should remain, that whatever you ask the Father in His Name, He would give it to you.

THE GREATEST CHOICE

In His Divine plan to provide His children a way of escape from sin, Almighty God sent His only Son to earth—to be born as a man and to die on the Cross for our iniquity. Our salvation is a matter of choice—God's and ours.

Scripture records: *"For God so loved the world, that he gave his only begotten Son* [God's choice] *that whosoever believeth in him* [our choice] *should not perish, but have everlasting life* [our reward]" *(John 3:16 KJV).*

I have met those who say, "It's wonderful that Jesus came to earth so that I can live with Him forever in Heaven!" They believe their future is the result of God's decision, not theirs. But that's not how salvation works. Of course Jesus shed His precious Blood on the Cross for you and me, but we must—with an act of our will—choose to ask Him to forgive us.

Scripture proclaims: *"if you confess with your mouth Jesus as Lord, and believe in your heart that God raised Him from the dead, you will be saved; for with the heart a person believes, resulting in righteousness, and with the mouth he confesses, resulting in salvation" (Romans 10:9-10).*

The most important choice God will ever ask you to make is to accept or to reject the gift of His Son—Jesus Christ—and to make Him the Lord of your life. The consequence of that choice determines *where* you're going to spend eternity. But other choices you make in life, your attitude and actions, unlock the door to God's rewards and determine *how* you're going to spend eternity.

TOTAL FORGIVENESS

There are many who believe that they can never be forgiven and reconciled to God because they have made such horrendous mistakes and bad choices that their actions are unpardonable.

A man recently said to me, "You know, Dave, the things I have done in my life are so bad I don't see how God could ever forgive me. So why should I even try to live a Christian life?" I assured him the Lord *can*—He *will*—and He *does*—forgive us when we repent and ask for His forgiveness. The Word declares: *"As far as the east is from the west, so far* hath he removed our transgressions from us" (Psalms 103:12 KJV). We also know, "If we confess our sins, he is faithful and just to forgive us our sins, and to cleanse us from all unrighteousness" (I John 1:9 KJV).

The Lord can certainly redeem our wrong choices. However, just because the Lord wipes our slate clean and gives us a new beginning does not mean we avoid the consequences of our past actions. Let's be realistic. The wrong we have done may not only affect us—it may affect others. Even when we are redeemed by His blood, our wrong choices can still affect our health, our reputation, and our right to be in leadership.

God absolutely will forgive our sins when we ask Him to! We have His Word on it! He is just and merciful. It's great to know that each and every morning, when we wake up and open our eyes, God renews His grace and mercy to us. I can tell you from personal experience, "The Lord's loving kindnesses indeed never ceases, for His compassions never fail. They are new every morning; Great is Your faithfulness" (Lamentations 3:23).

Regardless of your past, God's grace is sufficient—if. If we make the choice to turn from our sinful ways, humble ourselves, pray, seek His face and repent, His faithfulness toward us is great!

A HEART-CHANGING EXPERIENCE

Have you ever personally asked Jesus Christ to be the Lord of your life? If not, would you consider making this life-changing choice today? If so, I'd love for you to pray these simple words with me:

"Heavenly Father, I come before You now in the name of Your Son Jesus, asking You to forgive me for my sins. Come *into my heart and be the Lord and Savior of my life. I believe You are the Son of God. I believe You died on the cross and shed Your Blood for my sins. I believe You rose from the grave, conquering death and hell for all Eternity. Make me Your child right now. Wipe away my past and give me a whole new beginning. Lord, create in me a strong desire to study Your Word and spend time talking with You and worshiping You so I will grow and mature in my relationship with You. I ask and receive this, in the name of Jesus Christ. Amen."*

Thank You, Lord!

Without question, asking Jesus Christ to forgive your sins, come into your heart and become the Lord of your life is the most important decision you will ever make. It is a heart-changing experience that, with the guidance of the Holy Spirit, will help you make the best possible choices for the rest of your life.

BIG DOORS SWING ON SMALL HINGES

*Large streams from
little mountains flow;
tall oaks from little acorns grow.*

DAVID EVERETT

People thought Wilbur and Orville Wright were crazy! The two brothers from Ohio had traveled all the way to Kitty Hawk, North Carolina, to test a contraption they believed could rise above the earth and actually fly.

On a cold, windy morning in December 1903, after three days of failure, the Wrights "aeroplane" made it off the ground for 12 seconds—flying just 120 feet. They repeated their efforts throughout the day—finally hovering above the ground for 59 seconds and traveling 852 feet.

That doesn't sound like much of an achievement, yet for the first time man had defied the pull of gravity in a heavier-than-air craft. That small beginning transformed our world in ways no one could have imagined at the time.

Many years later, on July 20, 1969, Neil Armstrong stepped out of the Apollo spacecraft and placed his foot on the moon, saying, "That's one small step for man, one giant leap for mankind."

What a long journey from Kitty Hawk to the moon!

BEYOND IMAGINATION

Many of the dramatic turning points of civilization didn't seem exceptional at the time:

• Who could have dreamed of the great reformation that occurred in the church after Martin Luther nailed his *95 Thesis* on the door of the Wittenberg Castle Chapel in 1517?

• On Christmas night, 1776, George Washington crossed the Delaware River and caught the British troops by surprise. It was a defining moment of the American Revolution that changed world history.

• In 1965, a computer in Massachusetts was connected with one in California through a low-speed, dial-up telephone line. Today the world communicates at lightning speed via the Internet.

UNEXPECTED EVENTS

When I talk with people about the memorable turning points of their lives, I am often amazed to hear how an insignificant event had major consequences. If you think for a moment, perhaps you can recall such an event in your life—a casual conversation with someone that resulted in a new, exciting career—an unexpected introduction that led to a permanent relationship.

This was certainly true for me. I was in a discount department store in Tulsa, Oklahoma, buying some materials to decorate my dorm room at Oral Roberts University when I struck up a conversation with the attractive checkout girl. You guessed it...she is now my wife, Barbara, and the mother of our children!

GETTING READY

Never ignore or minimize the minor assignments of life. If your pastor or employer asks you to help with a task, however small, do it cheerfully as unto the Lord. After all, He is aware of every action of our daily life and every motivation of our hearts.

Jesus declares: *"He who is faithful in a very little thing is faithful also in much; and he who is unrighteous in a very little thing is unrighteous also in much"* (Luke 16:10).

Your "ministry" may include cleaning the church kitchen in preparation for a family night or changing diapers in the nursery while the service is in progress. Remember, God knows exactly where you are and what you are presenting to Him. He often places you in a "boot camp," making you ready for an important assignment of His choosing. Don't overlook or underestimate God's question: *"For who has despised the day of small things?"* *(Zechariah 4:10)*

SMALL BUT MIGHTY!

The most powerful forces are often controlled by tiny objects we may never see. For example, James tells us to *"Look at the ships...though they are so great and are driven by strong winds, are still directed by a very small rudder wherever the inclination of the pilot desires"* (James 3:4).

James was emphasizing an important Biblical principle. In the next verse, he continues: *"So also the tongue is a small part of the body, and yet it boasts of great things. See how great a forest is set aflame by such a small fire!"* (v.5-6)

So often, we desire the biggest, the greatest and the highest. When the apostles learned the value of faith, they wanted more, asking Jesus: *"Increase our faith!"* (Luke 17:5) Listen to the Lord's reply: *"If you had faith like a mustard seed, you would say to this mulberry tree, 'Be uprooted and be planted in the sea'; and it would obey you"* (v.6).

When God is involved, a little is all that is needed.

TOO LITTLE?

The small village of Bethlehem may not have garnered much attention in its day, yet it would be where the greatest event of history would take place—where the Savior of the World would be born. Centuries before, God spoke through the prophet Micah, saying, *"But as for you, Bethlehem...Too little to be among the clans of Judah, from you One will go forth for Me to be ruler in Israel. His goings forth are from long ago, from the days of eternity"* (Micah 5:2).

To God, Bethlehem was not an obscure place, but a *holy* city.

ONLY A "MITE"

One day Jesus was in the Temple at Jerusalem watching the rich place their gifts into the treasury. Then He saw something that instantly caught His attention: a poor widow putting in two small copper coins called "mites" worth about one-third of a cent each.

The Lord responded with praise: *"Truly I say to you, this poor widow put in more than all of them; for they all out of their surplus put into the offering; but she out of her poverty put in all that she had to live on"* (Luke 21:3-4).

To this woman, it didn't matter that she wasn't dressed in the fashion of the day or that the leading members of the community ignored her presence. She went to the Temple with one objective: to worship the Lord with her giving, knowing He is no respecter of persons. And so she gave all the money she had to God.

To me, the exceptional part of the story is the fact Jesus was watching! I believe that at that precise moment, the Lord began preparing a great reward for this woman to receive one day.

THE MULTIPLICATION FACTOR

Many would maintain, "Since I have practically nothing to give, why should I give at all? What difference can it make?" My friend, the small thing God has placed in your hand is awesome when it is combined with the power of the Almighty God!

• The widow at Shunem had nothing in her house but a jar of oil. Yet, because of her faith and obedience to the Prophet Elisha's words, God multiplied what she had given and worked a miracle of provision. Every available vessel was suddenly filled to the brim, and the Prophet said, *"Go, sell the oil and pay your debt, and you and your sons can live on the rest"* (II Kings 4:7).

• Young David only had five smooth stones for his slingshot when he came against the mighty Goliath. But that's all the Lord needed. The Bible records that when David slung the first stone, it *"struck the Philistine...And the stone sank into his forehead, so that he fell on his face to the ground"* (I Samuel 17:49). Many people pass over the point that David selected *five* smooth stones from the brook. However, this wasn't because he expected to miss the mark the first time. Did you know that Goliath had four brothers? He did! You can read the story in Scripture (II Samuel 21). When David chose those five stones, it was as though he were saying, "Goliath this one is for you! And I've got four more for your brothers!" David trusted God's faithfulness to work through him and bring about the victory!

• When Jesus was speaking to a large crowd on the shore of Galilee and lunchtime approached, one of His disciples said, *"There is a lad here who has five barley loaves and two fish, but what are these for so many people?"* (John 6:9) From such meager resources, the Lord miraculously fed 5,000.

ONE TINY WORD!

As you study God's Word you soon realize that your

entire future hinges on one of the shortest words in the Bible: "*IF.*"

Our Heavenly Father desires to enter into Divine Covenants with us and fulfill great promises to us, yet His Covenants are conditional. Again and again, He announces that *if* we do our part—*then* He will do His part.

In Chapter Two we talked about how choices bring rewards. Let's take a closer look at the blessings and curses resulting from the choices we make. God told the people through His servant, Moses: "*Now it shall be, if you diligently obey the Lord your God, being careful to do all His commandments which I command you today...All these blessings will come upon you and overtake you*" (*Deuteronomy 28:1-2*).

THE BLESSINGS

Listen to just a few of God's promises from Deuteronomy 28 that you can claim *IF* you choose to obey Him:
- The Lord will set you high above all the nations of the earth *(v.1)*.
- You will be blessed in the city and in the country *(v.3)*.
- Your offspring will be blessed *(v 4)*.
- Your herds will be increased *(v.4)*.
- "*Blessed shall you be when you come in, and blessed shall you be when you go out*"(v.6).
- Your enemies will flee (v.7).
- The Lord will bless everything you put you hand to (v.8).
- Your land will be blessed (v.8).
- "*The Lord will establish you as a holy people to Himself*" (v.9).
- You will abound in prosperity (v.11).

- The Lord will *"open for you His good storehouse, the heavens, to give rain to your land in its season"* (v.12).
- You will be a lender, not a borrower (v.12).
- *"The Lord will make you the head and not the tail, and you only will be above, and you will not be underneath"* (v.13).

This is the *good* news!

THE CURSES

Now listen to a few of God's promises from Deuteronomy 28 that will happen *IF* you choose to *disobey* Him:

- *"But it shall come about, if you do not obey the Lord your God, to observe to do all His commandments and His statutes with which I charge you today, that all these curses will come upon you and overtake you"* *(v.15).*
- *"Cursed shall you be in the city, and cursed shall you be in the country"* *(v.16).*
- Your offspring will be cursed *(v.18).*
- Your crops and herds will be cursed *(v.18).*
- *"Cursed shall you be when you come in, and cursed shall you be when you go out"* *(v.19).*
- You will have confusion and rebuke in everything you undertake *(v.20).*
- You will have pestilence and ill health *(vv.21-22).*
- *"The Lord will make the rain of your land powder and dust"* *(v.24).*
- *"Your carcasses will be food to all birds of the sky and to the beasts of the earth, and there will be no one to frighten them away"* *(v.26).*
- You will be oppressed and robbed continually, with no one to save you *(v.29).*

- These curses *"shall become a sign and a wonder on you and your descendants forever"* (v.46).
- *"The Lord will bring a nation against you from afar...a nation whose language you shall not understand"* (v.49).
- You will be scattered throughout the earth (v.64).

What a stark, contrasting set of rewards, all of which are the outcome of how you choose to respond to the word "if"!

SMALL CHOICES BRING SIGNIFICANT RESULTS

Moses is another great example to us. The children of Israel needed water—after all, three million people in the hot desert required plenty to drink. God said to Moses, *"Speak to the rock"* (Numbers 20:8).

If you recall the story, you may remember that Moses struck the rock with his rod. Some people read the story and think Moses' disobedience was that he struck the rock strike twice instead of once. That's not correct. God had told Moses to *speak* to the rock.

Because Moses was angry with the people, he instead *chose* to disobey God and *struck* the rock. What was the consequence of that seemingly small and insignificant choice of disobedience? Moses forfeited his role of leadership—and lost his right to enter the Promised Land of milk and honey.

Oh, the consequences of that small act! God, said, "Moses, you're not going to enter the Promised Land. Instead, Joshua will lead My people there" (v. 12).

Friend, what may seem like a small or trivial choice can keep you from the destiny God has chosen for you!

THE DOMINO EFFECT

Don't allow what may seem to be a minor decision to develop into a fire raging out of control. Left unattended, just one character flaw can mushroom into a crisis.

The Lord doesn't cause the problem—we do. James tells us what can happen when we choose to indulge in only one temptation. He writes: *"Let no one say when he is tempted, 'I am being tempted by God;' for God cannot be tempted by evil, and He Himself does not tempt anyone"* *(James 1:13).* The decision to sin is ours.

Even more dangerous, what begins as a trivial matter can take on a domino effect, triggering consequences that grow progressively worse. For example: *"But each one is tempted when he is carried away and enticed by his own lust. Then when lust has conceived, it gives birth to sin; and when sin is accomplished, it brings forth death"* *(James 1:14-15).*

This destructive path leads to doom: lust—sin—death. And it all begins when we choose to yield to temptation.

THE UPWARD TRAIL

Let's travel a more satisfying route—one that leads from where we are to the place where God desires for us to be. Peter writes: *"Now for this very reason also, applying all diligence, in your faith supply moral excellence, and in your moral excellence, knowledge, and in your knowledge, self-control, and in your self-control, perseverance, and in your perseverance, godliness, and in your godliness, brotherly kindness, and in your brotherly kindness, love"* *(II Peter 1:5-7).*

These spiritual attributes are not to remain stagnant,

but are to multiply and expand: *"For if these qualities are yours and are increasing, they render you neither useless nor unfruitful in the true knowledge of our Lord Jesus Christ" (v.8).*

When you reach your final destination, Jesus desires to say to you: *"I know your deeds, and your love and faith and service and perseverance, and that your deeds of late are greater than at first" (Revelation 2:19).* Don't focus on your less-than-stellar beginnings. They are in the past. Start *"reaching forward to what lies ahead" (Philippians 3:13).*

The Lord stands waiting beside a door of great promise. He invites you to enter.

HOW CHOICES AFFECT YOUR PERSONAL LIFE

He who chooses the beginning
of a road chooses the place it leads to.
It is the means that determines the end.

HARRY EMERSON FOSDICK

Barbara and I have lost count of the number of women who have said to us, "I made a choice to marry a man. He loved me, but he didn't know the Lord. I knew the Bible told me not to be unequally yoked together with an unbeliever, but I loved him, and I thought it would all work out. I thought God would speak to his life through me and I could change him." Years later, she is crying, "Oh, Lord, if only I had listened to You. If only I had obeyed Your Word and not married an unbeliever!" Their marriage ends in shambles with much pain and sadness.

How many people—and not just the young—in the height of some emotional moment choose to engage in sexual promiscuity? "Oh, one time won't hurt." But it does hurt. "No one will ever know." But somehow, they are found out. "God will forgive me." And He will. But what about the consequences?

In one moment, an unwanted pregnancy occurs and the "perfect" plan of God is thwarted. Often the reward… the consequences…is a ruined future, and the "wages" of their sinful decision will be paid for a lifetime!

Yes, God can forgive you. Yes, God can bring good out of a wrong choice. He can cover you with His mercy, grace and forgiveness. But often the consequences aren't very easy to deal with.

It's so important for young and old alike to decide what standards they will set for themselves regarding dating, courtship and marriage. They need to answer these questions early in the relationship:

- What are the boundaries we will not cross?
- Do we want our relationship to meet the standards of God's Word?
- Do we want our behavior to be pleasing in the Lord's sight?

THE PRICE OF FRIENDSHIP

Parents plead with their teens, "Make the right choices in selecting your circle of friends"—yet kids often have difficulty understanding this warning. They don't realize the dangers lurking ahead.

We know a family whose son has become friends with a group of young men who are on the wrong side of the law. These "friends" are involved in gangs, drugs and robbery.

"Oh, don't worry," the boy said, "I know where to draw the line. These guys are really fun to be around. Underneath, they're okay!" But the price of friendship sometimes isn't worth the risk.

I had a chance to speak to this teen and seized the opportunity to warn him: "As long as you hang around with these individuals and make them your friends, you're playing with fire. Their environment and influence on you will be much stronger than you can imagine."

I could see the consequences ahead and cautioned him: "Before you know it you'll be drawn into what they are doing because you'll want to be part of the group. And frankly, the time will come when your continued association with them will be dependent on your doing certain things to prove your loyalty to them. There will come a day when you run out of options. Choosing to be part of a gang is not a halfway commitment. You're either 'in' or you're 'out.'"

Later, when the young man left, all I could do was pray for God's protection over him and ask God to somehow get a hold of him and turn his life around.

IS IT CONTAGIOUS?

You may not be faced with a situation as serious as the

association of gang members, yet the people with whom you surround yourself and the friends you choose are crucial.

Do you choose to stay in the company of people who are negative, complaining, and constantly unhappy? Are these the individuals you allow to speak into your life?

This is a vital decision for you to make: You can decide to remain in such relationships, or you can back away, praying that God will help change their pessimistic outlooks.

The Bible speaks often concerning holiness—and *unholiness.* Unfortunately, many God-fearing people believe that holy living is contagious. It's not. They think, "If I live a righteous life before the world, unbelievers will be drawn to me and come to know the Lord."

Of course, in order to win people to Christ, you need to have communication with them, yet you should not make them your close buddies. Paul warned: *"Do not be bound together with unbelievers; for what partnership have righteousness and lawlessness, or what fellowship has light with darkness?" (II Corinthians 6:14).*

According to the Bible, if you touch something spiritually unclean, *you* can become spiritually unclean. Your purity can be contaminated—not the other way around. As Job asked, *"Who can make the clean out of the unclean?" (Job 14:4)*

This same parallel of truth is found in the physical world. Take a look at something as simple as an infection. If you are exposed to a bacteria or disease, you can easily become infected and then transmit the bacteria to someone else.

I've heard the excuse, "I stay around this person because I'm hoping he will change." Wishing, hoping and even praying is fine, but don't allow your life to be tarnished by associating with others who clearly are living outside of God's will.

ERECTING BARRIERS

God knew exactly what He was doing when He designed and created man:

- He made us with eyelids so that we can shut out what we don't need to see.
- He designed our neck so that we can turn away from evil.
- He fashioned our mouth so that we could close our lips and avoid speaking what is harmful to others.

Sadly, most people have not placed filters or erected barriers regarding what they choose to watch on television, the movies they attend, the books and magazines they read, or the lyrics of music they allow to enter their mind.

Perhaps you flip on the television and leave it on as background noise during your daily routine. Let me assure you; it is much more than "noise." Scripture tells us *"words...are spirit, and they are life" (John 6:63)*. We also know that

"Death and life are in the power of the tongue" (Proverbs 18:21).

Why does this matter? If you choose to watch an immoral television program, that same spirit permeates the air—and will invade *your* spirit.

You may be casually watching TV and say, "Oh, that sounds interesting." At first there may not be anything suggestive in the program—then, wham, there it is!

What do many of us do? We think, "This scene will be over in just a moment. Let's get past this garbage so I can see the end of the program." We tolerate the bad, hoping to return to the good.

Some even exclaim, "Oh, isn't that terrible! I can't believe what they're doing on TV!" Yet, they stay glued to the screen, complaining the entire time. It is far better to take the remote control in your hand and with one "click," say, "I'm not watching that!" Or, if you are reading a novel that is peppered with filthy language and trashy innuendos, close the book and throw it away!

THE INVASION

So many Christians wonder, "Why am I in such a spiritual battle all the time?" not realizing the depths of the invasion that has taken place. They have made a *choice*. Even without associating physically with ungodly people, they have allowed Satan to creep into their mind and spirit.

The moment we welcome wickedness—whether through a personal relationship or an inanimate object such as a television, we become friends with evil. King Jehoshaphat was asked, *"Should you help the wicked and love those who hate the Lord and so bring wrath on yourself from the Lord?" (II Chronicles 19:2).* I believe you already know the answer.

Let's follow the example of King David, who declared, *"I will set no wicked thing before mine eyes" (Psalm 101:3).*

WHERE'S THE CONTROL?

The Lord does not turn a blind eye to the actions of His people. He is watching us as individuals and as a nation. When we abandon self-control and become more concerned with personal gratification than glorifying

God, there is trouble on the horizon. Scripture tells us: *"For the Lord humbled Judah because of Ahaz king of Israel, for he had brought about a lack of restraint in Judah and was very unfaithful to the Lord"* (II Chronicles 28:19).

Does this verse sound familiar? I think we can conclude that we are experiencing a lack of restraint across this nation.

DRAWING THE LINE

I'm sure you have heard the saying, "You are what you eat." Research tells us we also become what we watch and listen to. Our style, language and behavior are often shaped by what we see and hear through the media.

It is vital that we make a conscious effort to filter out anything that does not uplift or build our spirit man. We need to monitor both the quantity and the quality of the information entering our homes and our very beings. The Apostle Paul wrote, *"All things are lawful, but not all things are profitable. All things are lawful, but not all things edify"* (I Corinthians 10:23).

As I wrote in my book *Turn Off the Darkness,* God has given us the discernment to know right from wrong. He expects us to take charge of the environment in our homes and lives. We must set guidelines regarding the...

...places we go.

...things we do.

...what we listen to.

...what we watch.

Dozens of times each day we all make choices regarding what will or will not be part of our lives. We must have the spiritual fortitude to draw a line of demarcation between good and evil.

DOES THE LORD APPROVE?

We've been talking about how decisions affect our personal relationships and the importance of staying pure before God, yet at every stage of our growth and development, we are grappling with choices. For example:

- Do I treat my body as the temple of the Holy Spirit?
- Do I care for my health, eating the right foods and exercising?
- What choices do I make to develop my gifts and talents?
- What decisions do I make to control my emotions?
- How do my choices will affect my reputation?
- How do I avoid the "appearance of evil"?
- What ethical choices do I make at work?

You may ask, "David, what is the most important thing I should consider when making personal decisions?" Let me answer by giving you an example from the Bible. King Jotham was only 25 years old when he began reigning over Jerusalem, and he ruled the city for 16 years. What was the secret of his success? The Bible records, *"Jotham became mighty because he ordered his ways before the Lord his God"* (*II Chronicles 27:6*). He determined to model his life after the Almighty and was highly favored.

A few years ago there was a national campaign to promote the acronym WWJD—What Would Jesus Do? The letters adorned bracelets, t-shirts, bumper stickers and posters. Here is a question we should continue to ask ourselves daily: **"Do my actions have God's Divine stamp of approval?"**

HOW CHOICES AFFECT YOUR FAMILY

*A man ought to live so that
everybody knows he is a Christian—
and most of all, his family ought to know.*

DWIGHT L. MOODY

All people on earth have this in common: *we have all been children*. And we know firsthand how the decisions made by our parents have shaped and directed our lives.

Earlier I told you how I had to come to grips with the fact that my father was rarely home because of his call to international evangelism. Rather than becoming distraught and bitter, I chose to accept the call of God on Dad's life and on our family. Yet, deep in my heart I always thought, "When I grow up, it's going to be different. I'm not going to be away from my family."

Even though my focus was on the business side of the ministry, I found myself traveling more than I would have liked. Suddenly, I was faced with the same choice that my father had to make many years ago: Would I be willing to sacrifice time with my family to be in ministry? It wasn't an easy decision.

However, when Barbara and I decided to have a family, I determined to be a stay-at-home dad as much as possible in order to give my children the time and attention they deserved.

Did that decision mean I would have perfect teenagers who would never rebel and never cause us heartache or pain? Absolutely not. We were faced with the same challenges millions of parents experience. Nonetheless, this was a *choice* that I believed God was calling me to make for our family, and I have never regretted it.

As a father, I have learned that when I obey the Lord, He rewards both me AND my family with His blessings.

THE RIGHT DECISION

In 1990 Barbara and I uprooted our family and moved

from San Diego to Charlotte to become stewards of The Inspiration Networks. Without question, it was a pressure-filled, traumatic time—especially for our children who had to leave their friends behind. Yet, Barbara and I prayerfully weighed the options and believed in our hearts we had made the right decision.

At that point in my life, God had given me many wonderful experiences—both in my spiritual life and in the corporate world. I had years of broadcast experience. I knew television production, understood media equipment, and knew how to design and build TV facilities. Although there were plenty of miles on my life's speedometer, I was the first to admit I didn't know the world of cable television. As I told a friend, "I didn't know Cable from Mabel!"

However, the decision had been made, and I totally immersed myself into the fascinating new arena of broadcasting. And what a baptism of fire it was!

THE VISION

It wasn't long before I began to hear God speaking to me about using the media as tool to reach people for Christ. So much of Christian television was "by Christians, for Christians, and about Christianity," but where was the evangelism? What about the Lost? I began to see that most Bible-centered television had become a great "keeper of the aquarium" but not a very effective "fisher of men."

I saw how the media—and television in particular—had taken center stage in our culture—probably becoming the most powerful force in the past 50 years. For better or for worse, television shapes and molds the minds and behavior of the billions of viewers who watch it.

Because of the decision we had made and our willingness to listen to the voice of the Master, He began giving me a vision. I started seeing television as a vital tool for discipleship and evangelism—a tool to be used by God to impact the values, beliefs, behavior, attitude and lifestyles of millions for His Kingdom—especially children and young people.

Praise God, it is happening! Since we launched these efforts in 1990, we have watched the Lord take this network from being available in barely three million homes to now being available in over 27 million homes. We've grown from five employees to over 250—from one network to three. But the most important fact is the thousands of lives being changed: families reunited, marriages restored, physical bodies healed, and Souls saved. We thank God for these victories.

The Lord also answered the cries of our hearts for our children, Ben and Becky. Today they both are married, raising their own families, and serving God.

These past years have not been without problems, but God has always been faithful. I learned firsthand that He is a Rewarder of those who diligently seek Him (Hebrews 11:6). These blessings are the direct consequences of choices Barbara and I made.

"HERE AM I!"

About three years ago, Barbara and I began to feel the Lord asking us to make another life-changing choice. God wanted to know, "Are you willing to step outside your comfort zone in the world of business and move into direct, personal ministry?"

Oh, if you only knew how much I chaffed at that

thought! I became an ordained minister in 1974, but my "ministry" was business. The Lord had blessed me with abilities in that area, and I felt comfortable. Yes, my life involved God's work, yet always in a supportive role—rarely in a pulpit. I wrestled with God. "Why? Why me? Why now? Ask someone else."

Perhaps you remember the Bible story when God called Samuel. When the young boy heard the voice of the Lord, he answered, *"Here am I" (I Samuel 3:4).*

This was also my response. I know I have made mistakes and failed my Heavenly Father many times, yet I know that I can honestly look God in the face someday and say, "Lord, whenever I heard Your call, whenever You placed a choice before me, I answered 'Yes!' I have never knowingly disobeyed something I felt You specifically calling me to do."

Now I was saying again, "Here am I, Lord. I will answer Your call." The result of that decision was for Barbara and me to launch a weekly television program, *Changing the World.* Once more, the Lord rewarded our choice. In the last few years, we have received literally thousands of testimonies from people asking us to agree with them in prayer.

Have you ever noticed how God's will seems to be progressive? When we answer, "Yes" to one assignment, He opens the next door to the next. The Lord doesn't reveal the whole picture all at once; He guides us one step at a time.

ANOTHER CHOICE

Recently, the Lord asked us to make yet another decision—one that would lead to an even greater involvement in personal, direct ministry. He was asking us to change our weekly program into a daily outreach. Again, I wrestled with God.

I thought about the growth process that we have been through as the Lord has given Barbara and me an enormous love for people. We have a great desire to see individuals equipped and empowered for successful living in Christ so that they will know the joy, peace, provision and blessing of the Lord and experience healing in their family relationships, finances, physical bodies and spiritual lives.

Our children are grown. We are grandparents and just getting to the point in life when we can enjoy one another more. And now a *daily* program? I kept asking, "God, why us? Why now?"

Few people can understand or appreciate what it takes to oversee a ministry such as The Inspiration Networks—the time, the personal sacrifice, the cost. I questioned, "Lord, can't we accomplish this with a weekly program? Yet, when Barbara and I knelt before the Lord, we felt His clear direction. He was saying, "Go!"

I am sharing all of this with you to emphasize this point: I am convinced that because we have made *choices* to obey God through the years, He has *rewarded* us by pouring out His abundant blessings on us, our children, and the ministry to which we have been called.

WISE COUNSEL

I had two great examples growing up: my mother and father. The choices they made Sowed Seed into my life and taught me how to make God-honoring choices.

By your example and the decisions you make, you are Sowing Seed into your children that will produce a lifetime of rewards. We see that evidenced throughout the

Word. King David is one of many such examples. He *chose* to Sow Seed into his son Solomon (I Chronicles 22:12). The Seed David had Sown into Solomon—the words that David had spoken to his son—caused Solomon to respond to God one day by saying, "Give me wisdom." He didn't come up with that response to God all on his own. Long before God ever said to Solomon, "Ask what I shall give you" (II Chronicles 1:7), David had Sown Seed into his son's heart and mind.

When Solomon answered: *"Give Your servant an understanding heart to judge Your people to discern between good and evil. For who is able to judge this great people of Yours?"* (v. 10), the Lord was more than pleased with Solomon's answer.

God told Solomon that because he had not requested riches, long life, or the defeat of his enemies, He would not only give him wisdom, but He would bless him with much more. God declared: *"I have also given you what you have not asked, both riches and honor, so that there will not be any among the kings like you all your days"* (v.11-12).

The Seeds that you *choose* to Sow into your children will bring a lifetime of rewards for them as well—either for good or bad. I can confidently tell you that the wise counsel of a Godly father pays great dividends!

ARE YOU AN EXAMPLE?

You can't just talk the talk with your children—you must walk the walk before them! For example, you can speak to your child about the dangers of drugs and immorality until you are blue in the face, yet if you are living in sin, your child will follow your example, not your words.

Even more, your *hidden* iniquities—the sins you think no one knows about—will affect the lives of those you love for generations to come. You may find forgiveness, yet these transgressions still will impact your children. That's not my opinion, but God's declaration. The Word clearly states: *"The Lord is slow to anger and abundant in loving kindness, forgiving iniquity and transgression; but He will by no means clear the guilty, visiting the iniquity of the fathers on the children to the third and the fourth generations"* (Numbers 14:18).

Today, ask God to help you live a blameless life before your family—setting a Godly example—and Sowing Seeds of wisdom and righteousness into their lives.

TESTING THE BOUNDARIES

You may ask, "How should I respond when I've done my best, yet my children still make harmful choices?"

Don't panic! Regardless of how much you try to perfectly raise your kids, they will test your boundaries and cause sleepless nights. But remember, they are your children—your flesh and blood. We don't "disown" them because we disagree with the decisions they make! They are not the first to make mistakes and, sadly, they won't be the last. We all have made poor choices—including great men of God like David and Peter.

The best advice you can give you children (and yourself!) is to encourage them to repent sincerely before God for their sins and start over again. Just because a person fails once doesn't mean they are doomed to repeat the pattern. Talk about it with them! Pray about it together! Encourage them to make better choices next time.

If people never failed, God would not have spent so

much time teaching us about His grace and mercy. These free gifts from the Father are for imperfect people who make wrong decisions and need to be restored.

FIVE CHOICES FOR PARENTS

Here are five specific choices you can make to help build a strong foundation for your sons' and daughters' lives:

1. Choose to instill God's Word.

Some parents have the attitude, "My children will read the Bible when they're ready." That's not how the Lord intends for Scripture to be taught. It must start early—initiated by *you!* The Bible says: *"You shall teach them* [God's instructions] *diligently to your sons and shall talk of them when you sit in your house and when you walk by the way and when you lie down and when you rise up"* (Deuteronomy 6:7).

By Sowing the Word into your son or daughter, you are preparing for an Eternal Harvest. As Paul wrote to Timothy: *"From childhood you have known the sacred writings which are able to give you the wisdom that leads to salvation through faith which is in Christ Jesus"* (II Timothy 3:15). What a priceless gift from God!

2. Choose to teach your children to obey the Lord.

More than once, I've heard a mother warn her youngster, "You'd better obey me!" It's much more effective to teach the child the necessity of obeying the principles God has written in His Word. Through Moses, God told His people to *"return to the Lord your God and obey Him with all your heart and soul according to all that I command you today, you and your sons"* (Deuteronomy 30:2). Teach your child that obedience to God brings great rewards!

3. Choose to discipline your children in love.

Many parents carry the admonition to "spare the rod and ruin the child" to an extreme. As a result, their kids are beat up rather than brought up! Listen to what the Apostle Paul recommends: *"Fathers, do not provoke your children to anger, but bring them up in the discipline and instruction of the Lord"* (Ephesians 6:4).

At the same time, don't believe the pseudo-psychologists who tell you, "If you are too hard on your children, they will lose all respect for you." It's just the opposite. As Scripture declares: *"Furthermore, we had earthly fathers to discipline us, and we respected them; shall we not much rather be subject to the Father of spirits, and live?"* (Hebrews 12:9). Godly training and loving correction are the twin pillars of character.

4. Choose to pass on wisdom and knowledge.

The Bible tells you to *"keep your soul diligently, so that you do not forget the things which your eyes have seen and they do not depart from your heart all the days of your life; but make them known to your sons and your grandsons"* (Deuteronomy 4:9). As a child of God, you have been given a great heritage. Pass it on!

5. Choose to give both instruction and direction.

Don't ignore the wisdom of Solomon. *"Train up a child in the way he should go; even when he is old he will not depart from it"* (Proverbs 22:6). And what does God expect from someone who would be a leader in the church? *"He must be one who manages his own household well, keeping his children under control with all dignity"* (I Timothy 3:4). You only have one chance to raise a child. Make it count!

"LIKE A CHILD"

My heart is always touched when I read the story of

how Jesus reached out to children. I can picture the scene of parents bringing their young sons and daughters to Him just so that He could touch them.

However, the disciples—perhaps trying to protect the Lord from the crowd—rebuked those who brought the children. But when Jesus saw what the disciples were doing, "*He was indignant and said to them, 'Permit the children to come to Me; do not hinder them; for the kingdom of God belongs to such as these*" (Mark 10:14).

Then Jesus taught this spiritual application: "*Truly I say to you, whoever does not receive the kingdom of God like a child will not enter it at all*" (v.15). Finally, the Lord took the children in His arms "*and began blessing them, laying His hands on them*" (v.16).

I pray the choices you make today and tomorrow regarding your children will be pleasing to God and in His perfect will. To be a Christian means to be Christ-like. As you walk in the Word, you not only are becoming the person He has planned for you to be, but you are shaping and influencing the lives of your children.

As King David chose to Sow wise Seeds into the life of his son Solomon, choose to Sow wise Seeds into your children. May you be able to say, "*I have no greater joy than this, to hear of my children walking in the truth*" (III John 4).

HOW CHOICES AFFECT YOUR FINANCES

God will not merely judge us
on the basis of what we gave,
but also on the basis of what we did
with what we kept for ourselves.

ERWIN W. LUTZER

I'm sure you've read the news accounts of people who lived a modest or even an austere life. Yet when they died, neighbors were shocked to learn they had accumulated great wealth—even millions of dollars. What was their secret? These individuals made some significant choices regarding their spending and saving habits.

The same principle applies to any enterprise we undertake. As author Peter Drucker observes, "Whenever you see a successful business, someone once made a courageous decision."

Take a moment to reflect on these important questions:

- Do you choose to operate on a budget and live within your means, or do you choose to get into bondage with debt?
- Do you choose to make wise financial investments and plan for the future—higher education, home, retirement, even vacations?
- Do you choose to give God your first fruits—your tithes and offerings—or do you choose to rob God (Malachi 3)?
- Do you choose to teach your children the value of money and God's principles of faithfully tithing the first fruits of their income, giving offerings to the Lord, and supporting His work?

A PERPETUAL PROMISE

Seedtime and Harvest is a principle designed by God. This is His plan—not one devised by ordinary man. What God established is true! For me, for you, for everyone!

After the flood, God made a promise to Noah. He declared, *"While the earth remains, **seedtime and harvest**,* *and cold and heat, and summer and winter, and day and night shall not cease" (Genesis 8:22).* This Divine law is a perpetual promise.

Talk to any farmer, and he will tell you that if you want to reap a harvest, you must first plant seed. As long as he holds the seed in his hand, he will never experience a harvest greater than what he is holding. The same principle of God's truth and wisdom applies not only to what we plant in the field, but to our finances and even our spiritual blessings.

Ask yourself, "If I'm clutching Seed in my hand, how can I ever expect to Reap a Harvest?" The answer is: you can't! You need to let the Seed go and let it grow!

WHAT WILL YOU REAP?

Through the Prophet Haggai, the Lord asks, *"Is the seed still in the barn? Even including the vine, the fig tree, the pomegranate and the olive tree, it has not borne fruit"* (Haggai 2:19).

There is a spiritual precept in "letting go" of your Seed and Sowing it into Good Ground. Paul writes, *"Whatever a man sows, this he will also reap"* (Galatians 6:7). You can't Sow hatred and expect to reap love. You can't Sow anger and bitterness and then wait for a Harvest of peace and contentment.

You determine the crop! Whatever you Sow you will Reap. Only when you release to Him what you are holding does God begin to move. What you have Sown He begins to multiply.

I know from experience that when I ask God for a bountiful Harvest, He requires more of me: more of my time, more of my family, more of *everything!*

DOES IT SEEM AS THOUGH YOUR HARVEST NEVER COMES?

There are many reasons we sometimes don't Reap the kind of Harvest we are expecting. One reason is found in the book of Haggai. God says that when you *choose* to look after your own things—after your own house and not after the things of God or His house—you'll Sow much but Harvest little.

- You'll eat, but not be satisfied.
- You'll put on clothing, but not be warm.
- You'll earn wages and find out that you put them into a purse with holes.
- God says: "I'll call for a drought on the labor of your hands."
- When you choose to hold on to your Seed instead of Sowing it, you'll never bear fruit.
- You'll be rewarded with no Harvest.

SUPERNATURAL PROVISION

During planting in the springtime, a farmer faces the uncertainties of the elements. Will the weather be kind to his crops and produce a great harvest, or will it destroy his efforts and result in ruin?

As Christians we also wonder what each year will bring. What will happen with the economy, the stock market, the unemployment rate, competition in the market place, and the unexpected financial burdens we didn't foresee? We can never be certain of anything but God!

This is why we need the Protective Hand of our Heavenly Father and His favor over our lives. The Lord expects us to be obedient to His Scriptural Principles as we tackle the tasks He has placed before us.

Think about it...besides prayer and fasting, what else can you do that will bring God's supernatural provision and protection to you life? The answer is: Sowing the Seed God has placed into your hands. When you do, this simple act of faith becomes a Covenant between you and God that will not be broken because God is *always* true to His Word.

You may ask, "How much should I Sow?" Let's turn the question around: How great is your need? How much do you want the Lord to bless and prosper you in both spiritual and earthly matters? The Apostle Paul declares: *"He who sows sparingly will also reap sparingly, and he who sows bountifully will also reap bountifully" (II Corinthians 9:6).*

TAKE AN INVENTORY

What is a Seed? It is a tiny beginning with a huge future. A Seed is anything that can become *more.* Seed can include your time, your love, your talent, your patience, your money, and your prayers. God has given you a storehouse of Seed, and you need to take inventory. Stop worrying about what you don't have and begin to see what you *do* have.

Just as tiny acorns become giant oak trees, what you already possess can become mighty. Recognize what God has stored inside you. Don't bury or hide it—use it!

If what you are Sowing is not producing the Harvest you desire, change the Seed you're Sowing. Invest your time in prayer. Ask the Holy Spirit to reveal what you have been given—supernaturally and naturally—and Sow these Seeds into the lives of others.

HEAVEN'S ECONOMY

God's way of thinking is certainly different from ours. Man says, "If you need something, hold on to what you have, and try to get even more." God maintains, "If you need something, give it away, and *I* will give you more!"

Let's look at how the Lord spells out His plan for provision: *"Give, and it will be given to you. They will pour into your lap a good measure—pressed down, shaken together, and running over. For by your standard of measure it will be measured to you in return"* *(Luke 6:38).*

If you need a friend, be a friend. If you need money, give money. If you need help, assist someone else. When you act according to this Scriptural Principle, the Lord pours blessings back into your life. Do you see why I prefer God's economy?

DON'T BE IN A HURRY!

Slow down! Be patient and wait long enough for your investment to produce the desired Harvest. The Bible says, *"The Lord is good to those who wait for Him, to the person who seeks Him"* *(Lamentations 3:25).* Your waiting reveals trust: *"It is good that he waits silently for the salvation of the Lord"* (v.26).

The delay may be painful, but there is a required season between Sowing and gathering the Harvest. Far too many people become discouraged and give up when they don't see immediate results. Rarely are the results immediate when there is a process involved. Jesus says, *"The soil produces crops by itself; first the blade, then the head, then the mature grain in the head"* *(Mark 4:28).*

Give your Seed enough time to produce a Harvest.

Harvests take time. No one plants rosebush seeds today and then expects to go out to the garden and pick roses tomorrow!

THE KEY TO PLENTY

Scripture is clear regarding supporting the work of the Lord with our giving.

When you choose to rob God of your tithes and offerings, you are rewarded with a curse. *"Will a man rob God? Yet you are robbing Me! But you say, 'How have we robbed You?' In tithes and offerings. You are cursed with a curse, for you are robbing Me, the whole nation of you!"* *(Malachi 3:8-9)*

But wait! By choosing to obey the Lord and Sowing your tithes and offerings into the storehouse of God, He will throw open the windows of Heaven and pour out blessings on you until they overflow (v.10). Even more, the Lord will *"rebuke the devourer"* so that the fruits of your land will not be destroyed (v.11).

When you make the decision to honor the Lord with your money—giving Him the first and best of what you have—you will always know plenty: *"Honor the Lord from your wealth and from the first of all your produce; so your barns will be filled with plenty and your vats will overflow with new wine"* *(Proverbs 3:9-10)*. Sowing is your choice: Reaping is God's reward!

WHAT IS GOD'S STOREHOUSE?

Many Christians today have difficulty understanding the concept of the storehouse of God. In the Old Testament, the storehouse was an actual storage room—

a part of the Temple—where various things were stored for the service of the Temple. When something was needed by the priests for use in the Temple, they went to the storehouse and retrieved it.

The storehouse is God's place of *supply*. How does this apply to you today and where you pay your tithes and offerings? Where are you spiritually *supplied*, fed and nourished? If this is your church—then your church is God's storehouse for you. If a particular radio or television ministry is a blessing to your spiritual life—then that is God's storehouse for you. If there is another ministry speaking into your life and bringing you spiritual supply—then that is God's storehouse for you.

If more than one place is spiritually *feeding* you, then each is entitled to a portion of your tithes according to the proportion of spiritual nourishment you are receiving from them. The reality is that most Christians today are spiritually fed and nourished from more than one storehouse. Each is deserving of a portion of our tithes.

Let me give you a parallel in the natural realm. If you go out to eat at a restaurant, where do you pay your bill? You pay your bill where you ate. You don't eat at one restaurant and then go across the street to another diner to pay your bill because your best friend owns that particular restaurant, and you want to help him out. That would be wrong. It's the same with your tithes.

HAVE FAITH IN GOD'S WORD!

It's not enough to simply read about the promises of God. It is critical that you have faith in God to bring His Word—His Living and written Word—to pass in the circumstances of your life.

One of the greatest examples of faith in the Bible is what took place in the life of Mary, the mother of Jesus. But where did Mary receive the faith to believe she would bear a child and that He would be the Son of God? This was unexpected news to her!

The Father was not relying on Mary's faith to work the miracle—and the Lord is not restricted by your level of faith to bring forth what is needed in *your* life. What God was depending on with Mary—and what God is counting on in your circumstances—is His Word! God does not leave His Word vulnerable to your level of faith. The Lord desires that you rely on, and place your total trust in, Scripture; do not depend on yourself, nor your level of faith, but rather only on His Word.

When the angel told Mary she was going to bring forth a Son, she did not doubt or hesitate; she simply accepted the news and agreed, *"May it be done to me according to your word" (Luke 1:38).* The angel came with a message from God, yet Mary had to receive it by faith in her own life. In effect, she responded, "I believe what you have said. Let God's Word be true for me even as you have spoken it!" This is the kind of expectant response God desires from us.

FIVE DIVINE PRINCIPLES

If your life is consumed by chasing material possessions and building your financial portfolio, stop for a moment to listen to these words of Jesus: *"For what will it profit a man if he gains the whole world and forfeits his soul? Or what will a man give in exchange for his soul?" (Matthew 16:26)* Instead of living according to the world's economic plan, start obeying these Divine Principles:

1. Giving to God must come first.

"*Honour the LORD with thy substance, and with the firstfruits of all thine increase: So shall thy barns be filled with plenty, and thy presses shall burst out with new wine*"(*Proverbs 3:9-10 KJV*).

2. When you choose to seek the Lord, God will abundantly bless you.

The Bible says concerning King Uzziah: "*As long as he sought the Lord, God prospered him*" (*II Chronicles 26:5*). And Jesus declares: "*But seek first His kingdom and His righteousness, and all these things will be added to you*" (*Matthew 6:33*). Instead of asking yourself, "What am I Reaping?" ask, "What am I seeking?"

3. Don't give the Lord your leftovers.

According to His Word, when you choose to give the Lord your second best... your leftovers...the things that aren't important to you...He is not pleased, and He will not accept your offering (Malachi 1:6-10). According to Scripture, we are commanded to bring to the Lord the *first* of what we receive.

4. Give with a clean, forgiving heart.

Jesus teaches that when we choose to bring an offering to the Lord when we are at war with our brother, God will refuse our gift. He declares, "*First be reconciled to your brother, and then come and present your offering*" (*Matthew 5:24*). The Master also tells us that if we opt to practice our righteousness before men to be noticed and applauded, we have no reward with our Father in Heaven (Matthew 6:1).

5. Every act of kindness is an investment in eternity.

When we decide to live for others rather than ourselves, we Reap great dividends. As Paul writes: "*Knowing that whatever good thing each one does, this he will receive back from the Lord" (Ephesians 6:8).* Your choice to make an investment in lives is a treasure more valuable than silver or gold.

"ENLARGE MY BORDER"

We can *position* ourselves to receive God's favor. There is a verse in the Old Testament many of us had overlooked until Bruce Wilkinson called attention to it in his wonderful book, *The Prayer of Jabez.*

The Bible records that Jabez *"called on the God of Israel, saying, 'Oh that You would bless me indeed and enlarge my border, and that Your hand might be with me, and that You would keep me from harm that it may not pain me!' And God granted him what he requested" (I Chronicles 4:10).*

Read that prayer again and you will see there are four vital parts to Jabez' request:

First: Jabez asks God to bless him.

Second: He asks the Lord to enlarge his territory, giving him more responsibility.

Third: He prays for God to stay close to Him.

Fourth: Jabez requests the Lord to protect him from pain and harm.

This is a prayer you can offer to God each day. When you do, you are asking your Heavenly Father to be at the center of every activity of your life and affirming that your total reliance is on Him.

Now for the best part! God not only received the prayer of Jabez, He rewarded him by granting his request! The Word declares: *"The prayer of the upright is His delight" (Proverbs 15:8).*

The Lord will bring choices and opportunities into your life. They may not always be easy, but I promise that if you will make the decisions God desires, you will experience an abundant life, filled with His rewards—now, AND in the life to come!

HOW CHOICES AFFECT YOUR SPIRITUAL LIFE

*The spiritually minded believer
makes his decisions on the basis of
eternal values and not on
the passing fads of society.*

WARREN W. WIERSBE

Have you ever been around people who are slaves to their schedule? Every minute of the week is accounted for, and they won't let *anything* interrupt their routine. Every moment is all written down—when they eat, sleep, work, exercise, watch their kids play soccer, go to a movie, turn on the television set or visit Grandma. And, if God is fortunate enough, they might even set aside time for church on Sunday morning. One man, holding a palm size electronic scheduler, told me, "I just don't know how I existed before I bought this thing!"

Many have *compartmentalized* their lives to such an extent that there is absolutely no time left for prayer, reading the Word or building a foundation of faith. It is time for us all to pause and take a fresh, introspective look at our priorities. Every day we make choices that affect our family, our social life and our finances, but what about our *spiritual life*? What are we doing that will bring a "God consciousness" to every event we undertake?

Rather than giving the Lord a few scattered minutes here and there, we need Him to be at the center of our thoughts and continually reflected in our actions.

Instead, we say, "I'm going to pray the first thing every morning." But God says: *"Pray without ceasing"* (I Thessalonians 5:17). We say, "I need to concentrate on making a living." However, Jesus says: *"But seek first His kingdom and His righteousness, and all these things will be added to you"* (Matthew 6:33).

The Spirit-led life comes from giving the Lord *everything*—your time, your talent, your today, your tomorrow. Our spiritual lives are not a part-time trivial pursuit!

START EARLY

You are a new creation in Christ—and now it's time to grow spiritually.

Let's look at the life of Jesus when He was on earth. Yes, He was the Son of God, yet He still had a desire to learn and gain wisdom. When He was only 12 years old, Jesus traveled with His family and a group of people from Nazareth to Jerusalem for the Feast of the Passover. On the way home after the event, Mary and Joseph realized that Jesus wasn't with them. Three days later, they found Him in the Temple courts *"sitting in the midst of the teachers, both listening to them and asking them questions"* (Luke 2:46).

When they found Him, Mary exclaimed, *"Son, why have You treated us this way? Behold, Your father and I have been anxiously looking for You"* (v. 48).

Young Jesus replied, *"Why is it that you were looking for Me? Did you not know that I had to be in My Father's house?"* (v.49) From that time forward, *"Jesus kept increasing in wisdom and stature, and in favor with God and men"* (v.53).

Jesus made a *choice* to learn everything possible about the things of God.

OH, THE POTENTIAL!

Let's contrast this with another Nazirite who was born with an awesome
potential for greatness. His name was Samson.

Even before he was born, an angel appeared and told his mother—who was barren and childless—that she would have a son set apart at birth: *"and he shall begin to deliver Israel from the hands of the Philistines"* (Judges 13:5).

We read how *"the child grew up and the Lord blessed him. And the Spirit of the Lord began to stir him"* *(vv.24-25).*

Samson was chosen by God to be a ruler and judge over the children of Israel. The Lord had a plan for his life—one of leadership, responsibility and position. He became a man of power, both in physical strength and national authority, who led Israel for 20 years. And what a reputation he enjoyed! Samson could tear lions apart with his bare hands (Judges 14:6) and defeat 1,000 men with the jawbone of a donkey (Judges 15:15).

A RUINED PLAN

Sadly however, Samson made some tragic choices that ruined him spiritually. He fell in love with a woman named Delilah, who then was offered money to discover and reveal the source of Samson's strength. He gave into the lust of the flesh, and, in a moment of weakness, told her everything, including this secret: *"A razor has never come on my head, for I have been a Nazirite to God from my mother's womb. If I am shaved, then my strength will leave me and I will become weak and be like any other man"* *(Judges 16:17).*

As Samson lay sleeping, Delilah shaved his head and alerted the Philistines. They rushed in, bound the shaven and weakened man with ropes, brought him to Geza where they gouged out his eyes, and forced him to grind grain in the prison house.

God had a glorious future for Samson, yet he threw it all away by making wrong decisions. His life ended when, with one final burst of his former power, he pulled down the pillars that supported a temple crowded with Philistines. It must have been quite a scene. Scripture records:

"the dead whom he killed at his death were more than those whom he killed in his life" (Judges 16:30).

Choosing sin and disobedience will blind and deceive you, taking you hostage and finally destroying your life. Oh, what a difference when we listen to the voice of the Lord and obey His commands. It is the Father who *"satisfies your years with good things, so that your youth is renewed like the eagle"* (Psalm 103:5).

SEEDS OF GROWTH

There is a direct connection between your choices and your spiritual growth—a "cause and effect" relationship. Here are a few examples:

By choosing to receive God's ultimate gift, you will grow in love.

It's almost impossible to fathom how much the Father cares for us. However, He demonstrated it when He sent His Son to earth. His Word tells us: *"In this is love, not that we loved God, but that He loved us and sent His Son to be the propitiation for our sins"* (I John 4:10).

When we receive Christ, we receive the gift of His love so that we can share it with those around us: *"Beloved, if God so loved us, we also ought to love one another"* (I John 4:11). As a result, the treasure God has placed within us multiplies.

By choosing to ask the Lord, you will grow in wisdom.

The first step to receiving is requesting! And the storehouse of an all-wise God is yours for the asking. James writes: *"But if any of you lacks wisdom, let him ask of God, who gives to all generously and without reproach, and it will be given to him."* (James 1:5). I encourage you to make this request: "Lord, You are the source of all knowledge and understanding, and I am asking for Your wisdom today."

By choosing to draw near to God, you will grow in grace and mercy.

There are no barriers to prevent us from approaching the Lord; His arms are outstretched. *"Therefore let us draw near with confidence to the throne of grace, so that we may receive mercy and find grace to help in time of need"* (*Hebrews 4:16*). **Whosoever will may come!**

By choosing God's road, you will grow in joy.

Your spiritual life is not designed to be one of drudgery or a daily grind. Rather, God's plan is for it to be just the opposite. The psalmist declares: *"You will make known to me the path of life; in Your presence is fullness of joy; in Your right hand there are pleasures forever"* (*Psalm 16:11*). That's why Paul tells us to rejoice in the Lord ALWAYS!

By choosing righteousness, you will grow in courage.

We were not born to cower in fear and retreat because of worry and anxiety. These are responses learned from living in a world of sin. God has a better plan: *"In righteousness you will be established; You will be far from oppression, for you will not fear; And from terror, for it will not come near you"* (*Isaiah 54:14*). Ask the Lord to clothe you in His truth and set your feet on the Solid Rock so that you can combat every anxiety and live in triumph.

By choosing to receive the Lord, you will grow in hope and expectation.

Redemption is not only to free us from sin but also to release us from negative thinking. As Paul declares: *"Christ in you, the hope of glory"* (*Colossians 1:27*).

Your source of optimism is not man-made—your source is *GOD!* Pray with the psalmist: *"My soul, wait thou only upon God; for my expectation is from him"* (*Psalms*

62:5). Remember, you are a child of promise—and that means you have a glorious future!

By choosing to act upon belief and trust, you will grow in faith.

Each of us has been given a *"measure of faith" (Romans 12:3)*, yet this doesn't mean our faith can't increase. The apostles said to the Lord: *"Increase our faith!" (Luke 17:5)*—which means faith can grow and develop!

Faith is the essential ingredient for a Spirit-filled life; we must live by it (Romans 1:17), walk by it (Romans 4:12), and use our faith to overcome the world (Ephesians 6:16).

DON'T LOOK BACK!

When you read the accounts of great battles—from Biblical times to modern warfare—you know that victory doesn't come when you decide to retreat. It's imperative to stay on the offensive. The same is true in your walk with the Lord. If we lay down our armor and stop moving forward, the opposite of spiritual growth occurs—we become discouraged, even powerless.

Don't ignore what God declares through the Prophet Isaiah who says *"woe"* to those, *"Who execute a plan, but not Mine, and make an alliance, but not of My Spirit" (Isaiah 30:1)*. God warns those who run to the world to seek refuge and safety that the result will be *"your humiliation" (v.3)*.

Spiritual decline is a direct result of our stubborn, self-centered choices. The Lord says: *"Because I called and you refused, I stretched out my hand and no one paid attention; And you neglected all my counsel and did not want my reproof; I will also laugh at your calamity; I will mock when your dread comes" (Proverbs 1:24-26)*.

"Refusing" and "neglecting" are choices we make.

Why blame God for the consequences when we have been given every opportunity to make life-changing decisions?

YOUR PRIORITY

My friend, there is no easy shortcut to Heaven, but if you're looking for a sure-fire path to spiritual growth, spend time every day in God's Presence. When you choose to make Him your top priority, you will know His peace, His blessing, and His provision!

In the Old Testament, the Presence of the Lord was represented by the Ark of the Covenant. In one instance, during King David's reign, *"the ark of God remained with the family of Obed-edom in his house three months; and the Lord blessed the family...and all that he had"* (I Chronicles 13:14).

Today, we don't have the physical Ark to which we can draw near and receive God's blessings. Yet something far better has occurred to bring us into the very Presence of the Lord. You see, when Christ died on the Cross, *"the veil of the temple was rent in twain from the top to the bottom"* (Matthew 27:51). Now we can come *"boldly unto the throne of grace, that we may obtain mercy, and find grace to help in time of need"* (Hebrews 4:16).

Believe it or not Friend, when you choose to spend time in the Presence of the Lord, one of the great consequences will be His blessing on your life. What God did for the household of *Obed-edom,* He will do for you! His Presence brings blessings!

He is worthy of our praise and worship.

During one of the great battles in Israel, King Jehoshaphat and the army of Israel were so outnumbered by the enemy they didn't stand a chance (II Chronicles 20:2).

What did Jehoshaphat do? God told him to appoint singers to go out ahead of the army to praise the Lord. The Bible records the miraculous result: *"When they began singing and praising, the Lord set ambushes against [those] who had come against Judah; so they were routed"* *(v. 22)*. What a lesson! When you choose to praise and worship God in the face of your adversity, victory comes.

Lifting our voices to the Lord should not be limited to a Sunday church service. We need to *continually* spend time in His Presence. When you face an impossibility and don't feel you stand a chance, start giving the Lord honor and praise. Worship Him. You'll be surprised what the Lord will do for you!

OUR DAILY BREAD

In the wilderness, God miraculously provided manna to the children of Israel for them to eat, but they were only to collect enough food for one day at a time. What was collected one morning became rotten the next with a stench so bad that it made the people sick. Only on the sixth day was there manna that lasted *two* days—because God wanted them to keep the Sabbath holy (Exodus 16:5).

Part of what God was trying to teach the children of Israel through the manna experience was to be dependent on Him *every day*. He also wants us to know that we can't live today on yesterday's provision, yesterday's word, yesterday's experience! We need fresh manna every day! A fresh word from the Lord. A fresh spiritual experience with Him! Jesus said, *"Give us this day our **daily bread"*** *(Matthew 6:11)*.

Regretfully, many Christians don't choose to spend time with the Lord daily in His Presence, in His Word, in prayer, or in worship. How can we expect to be fed and nourished by Him if we don't spend time with Him? This is why—whether you realize it or not—you may be starving to death spiritually. Your spiritual life is malnourished and lacking the power you need to live an overcoming life. This changes when we choose to faithfully spend time with the Lord every day!

GREAT EXPECTATIONS!

Spiritual growth is the result of *abiding* and *dwelling* with the Lord. That's a promise from God's Word: *"He who dwells in the shelter of the Most High will abide in the shadow of the Almighty. I will say to the Lord, 'My refuge and my fortress, My God, in whom I trust!'" (Psalm 91:1-2).*

What can you expect when you make the choice to trust completely in the Lord alone? He will…

…deliver you from Satan's snares (v.3).

…become your Refuge and Protection (v.4).

…remove the fear of terror (v.5).

…shield you from harm (v.6).

…send His angels to guard you (v.11).

…honor you (v.15).

…reward you with a long, satisfying life (v.16).

And that's just the beginning of what the Lord will do for you!

STRENGTH FROM ABOVE

Spending time reading God's Word daily is a form of spiritual exercise. We are *built up*—both in faith and in the knowledge of the Father—to the point that we are living examples of His strength and power.

This is what empowered the Prophet Elijah and gave him such confidence in his showdown with the 450 prophets of Baal on Mount Carmel. Elijah gave them an ultimate choice: *"How long will you hesitate between two opinions? If the Lord is God, follow Him; but if Baal, follow him"* (I Kings 18:21).

Here was only *one* man of God coming against hundreds of unbelievers, yet complete belief in the Almighty was required to even issue such a challenge! He announced: *"Now let them give us two oxen; and let them choose one ox for themselves and cut it up, and place it on the wood, but put no fire under it; and I will prepare the other ox and lay it on the wood, and I will not put a fire under it. Then you call on the name of your god, and I will call on the name of the Lord, and the God who answers by fire, He is God."* *(vv. 23-24)*. The people agreed.

The prophets of Baal tried first, but after pleading with their god from morning until noon, nothing happened. Elijah even taunted them, saying, *"Call out with a loud voice, for he is a god; either he is occupied or gone aside, or is on a journey, or perhaps he is asleep and needs to be awakened"* *(vv. 27)*. So Baal's prophets shouted louder, even slashing themselves with swords and spears until their blood flowed. And still there was no fire.

"AT YOUR WORD"

That same evening, Elijah repaired the altar. He took 12 stones—one for each tribe of Israel—and dug a trench around it. Then, after the wood and meat were in place, he asked that water be poured over the sacrifice, not just once, but *three times! (v.34)*.

The challenge had been made, and now it was God's

turn. At that moment, Elijah looked up to heaven and spoke one of the most powerful prayers recorded in Scripture: *"O Lord, the God of Abraham, Isaac and Israel, today let it be known that You are God in Israel and that I am Your servant and I have done all these things at Your word. Answer me, O Lord, answer me, that this people may know that You, O Lord, are God, and that You have turned their heart back again"* (vv.36- 37).

What happened next? God's fire fell and burned up the sacrifice, the wood, the stones, the soil and even the water in the trench. When the people saw this, they fell on their faces and cried, *"The Lord, He is God; the Lord, He is God"* (v.39).

My friend, are you hesitating today in your choice to serve God? Are you hesitating to embrace His plans and purposes for your life? Hebrews 3:15 says, *"Today if you will hear his voice, harden not your hearts, as in the provocation."* The choice is yours. The right choice will bring a lifetime of rewards, in this life AND in the life to come.

THE STARTING POINT

You may ask, "Where do I begin? How do I embark on my path to spiritual growth that God has planned for me?" Start with the nourishment of the Word. Listen to what Peter says: *"Like newborn babies, long for the pure milk of the word, so that by it you may grow in respect to salvation"* (I Peter 2:2). Read God's Word, study it, make it a disciplined part of your life, and your spiritual life will grow and become strong.

Next, develop a strong prayer life, getting to know your Heavenly Father through daily communion. Then, find a body of Believers with whom you can fellowship

and sit under Spirit-filled teaching. When you add praise, worship, spiritual accountability and righteous living, there's no cap or limitation to what the
Lord will do in your life!
It's *your* choice.

HOW YOUR DECISIONS CAN DEFEAT THE DEVIL

When you close your eyes

to the devil, be sure
it is not a wink.

JOHN C. CULP

Everybody makes mistakes, but only some take responsibility for their actions. "What was I thinking? How could I have done such a stupid thing?" From my observations, however, most people look for an excuse to blame anyone or anything other than themselves:

- A man pulled over for exceeding the speed limit asks the patrolman: "Where was the sign? I didn't see one posted!"
- A salesman caught padding his expense account says, "I was just trying to cover what it *really* cost me to make the trip."
- A student accused of plagiarizing part of a term paper, protests, "Was I supposed to write every word myself? I thought you wanted me to do some research!"

Eve was the first person to offer the excuse repeated by millions to this day: "The devil made me do it!" Is this true? Does Satan really exert that kind of power over you? Are your attitudes and actions really controlled by him? If so, what steps can you take to defeat this evil foe?

THE DECEIVER

Let's not fool ourselves—there is a real devil roaming the earth who is very much alive. "*Be of sober spirit, be on the alert. Your adversary, the devil, prowls around like a roaring lion, seeking someone to devour*" (I Peter 5:8).

Satan is called the "adversary"—and he certainly is, to both God and man. He brings sin, disease, fear, torment and death. The devil is also a deceiver. Jesus declared: "*He was a murderer from the beginning, and does not stand in the truth because there is no truth in him. Whenever he speaks a lie, he speaks from his own nature, for he is a liar and the father of lies" (John 8:44).*

How do we know that Satan is the author of sickness? Because Jesus *"went about doing good and healing all who were oppressed by the devil" (Acts 10:38).* He also delivered a woman *"whom Satan has bound for eighteen long years" (Luke 13:16).* Let there be no doubt: It is the devil who attacks our bodies, our souls and our minds.

SATAN'S SCHEMES

As much as some people would like to ignore this subject, the reality is that Satan still prowls the land seeking to establish his devious plans. Paul tells us to stay alert, *"Lest Satan should take advantage of us; for we are not ignorant of his devices" (II Corinthians 2:11).*

The devil delights in distracting our attention from the Lord. That's why we are warned: *"Do not love the world nor the things in the world. If anyone loves the world, the love of the Father is not in him" (I John 2:15).*

Satan also tries to fill our mind with confusion and uncertainty. Jesus asks, *"Why are you troubled, and why do doubts arise in your hearts?" (Luke 24:38)* Do you remember when Peter walked on the water and then began to sink? The Master immediately stretched out His hand to take hold of him, asking, *"You of little faith, why did you doubt?" (Matthew 14:31)*

Satan tries to delay your spiritual progress. When Paul was to present his defense of the Gospel to Felix, the governor became frightened and said, *"Go away for the present, and when I find time I will summon you" (Acts 24:25).* In the words of a German proverb, "When God says today, the devil says tomorrow."

DANGER AHEAD!

The highway patrol has a slogan to warn people what will happen to their license if they are caught driving while intoxicated: "Booze it and lose it!"

According to the Word of God, we can say much the same thing about sin: "Choose it and lose it!" When we select evil over righteousness, we are the losers—our prayers are not answered, and we are left without hope unless and until we repent before God. The people of Israel were *"defeated before an enemy, because they have sinned against You" (I Kings 8:33).*

Let me remind you again that we are accountable for our choices, whether they be virtues or vices. The Lord will *"reward the doer of evil according to his wickedness" (II Samuel 3:39).*

Now hear the *good* news! Jesus was sent to earth to foil and ruin the schemes and snares of Satan. According to the Word: *"The Son of God appeared for this purpose, to destroy the works of the devil" (I John 3:8).*

Even more, Christ came to confront Satan himself. Jesus was crucified, *"that through death He might render powerless him who had the power of death, that is, the devil" (Hebrews 2:14).* My friend, I want you to know that Jesus Christ's victory at Calvary makes it possible for every Believer to take authority over Satan.

PLACE SATAN ON NOTICE

If we give the devil one minute of our attention, that's 60 seconds too much. Instead, start treating him as the defeated foe he actually is. Listen to the words of Jesus: *"Behold, I have given you authority...over all the power of the enemy" (Luke 10:19).*

According to Scripture, you can put Satan on notice that you are exempt from his evil attacks *"because greater is He who is in you than he who is in the world"* (I John 4:4).

The next time the devil comes your way, don't flinch. You have been granted power from Heaven that will cause him to turn and run. How is that possible? *"Submit therefore to God. Resist the devil and he will flee from you"* (James 4:7).

The demons of hell are fearful of Jesus and depart when He commands them to leave. In one encounter, the demons cried to the Lord: *"What business do we have with each other, Jesus of Nazareth? Have You come to destroy us? I know who You are—the Holy One of God!"* (Mark 1:24). And then the demons fled!

The Holy Spirit will erect a barrier to stop Satan in his tracks. He won't be able to go any further. *"When the enemy shall come in like a flood, the Spirit of the Lord shall lift up a standard against him"* (Isaiah 59:19).

WE HAVE THE POWER!

It isn't just Jesus who is able to cast out demons. Look at what happened to a Believer named Phillip who traveled to Samaria to preach the Gospel of Christ. Reporting on that great revival, the Bible says, *"For in the case of many who had unclean spirits, they were coming out of them shouting with a loud voice; and many who had been paralyzed and lame were healed"* (Acts 8:7).

The Apostle Paul also took authority over the enemy. A woman *"possessed with a spirit"* taunted the missionary evangelist in one city. After several days of her harassment, Paul was so annoyed that he turned and said to the spirit in her: *"'I command you in the name of Jesus Christ* to come out of her!' And it came out at that very moment" (Acts 16:18).

God was performing "extraordinary miracles by the hands of Paul so that handkerchiefs or aprons were even carried from his body to the sick, and the diseases left them and the evil spirits went out" (Acts 19:11-12).

It should come as no surprise that the followers of Jesus—including you and me –have the Divine Power He possesses. Before His ascension into Heaven, the Master announced: "These signs will accompany those who have believed: in My name they will cast out demons, they will speak with new tongues; they will pick up serpents, and if they drink any deadly poison, it will not hurt them; they will lay hands on the sick, and they will recover" (Mark 16:17-18).

From my experience in ministry around the world, I can tell you that miracles are occurring as never before—just as the Lord declared. He said: "Truly, truly, I say to you, he who believes in Me, the works that I do, he will do also; and greater works than these he will do; because I go to the Father" (John 14:12).

DECLARE IT!

We have been given the same power today that is in the Lord Jesus. The Word confirms: "as He is, so also are we in this world" (I John 4:17). So go ahead and boldly declare, **"I can take authority over Satan!"** Why? Because:
- "God says I can."
- "I am covered with the blood of Jesus Christ."
- "I am filled with His Spirit."
- "God's Word is in my heart."
- "God sends angels to protect me."
- "I speak in the name of Jesus."

Why allow the devil to pester you any longer? If Jesus can cause him to flee, so can you!

SIX DECISIONS

Don't buy into the notion that you can get rid of Satan by ignoring him. It doesn't work! Instead, defeat him by making these six decisions:

1. *Decide to confront the devil with God's Word* (Matthew 4:1-11).
2. *Decide to deny Satan any opportunity* (Ephesians 4:27).
3. *Decide to resist the devil* (Ephesians 6:13).
4. *Decide to flee from temptation* (Luke 22:40).
5. *Decide to stay out of Satan's territory* (II Samuel 11:1-5).
6. *Decide to take authority over evil (Jude 1:9).*

What Jesus said to Peter, He is also telling you: *"What-ever you bind on earth shall have been bound in heaven, and whatever you loose on earth shall have been loosed in heaven" (Matthew 16:19).*

With Satan on the attack, we can't afford to sit idly by. Confront him, bind him, and cast him out!

AN EXTRAORDINARY BATTLE

By God's grace and the prayers and support of our faithful Partners, The Inspiration Networks are touching countless lives—both in the United States and in foreign nations. But I can tell you that Satan clashes with us over every cable household we attempt to enter and over every man, woman, boy or girl we reach with the Gospel.

You see, the battle in which we are engaged is not of

this world. As Paul states: *"For the weapons of our warfare are not carnal, but mighty through God to the pulling down of strongholds; Casting down imaginations, and every high thing that exalteth itself against the knowledge of God, and bringing into captivity every thought to the obedience of Christ"* (I Corinthians 10:4).

The only way for us to triumph in this conflict against the enemy is to put on the whole armor of God—*"so that you will be able to stand firm against the schemes of the devil"* (Ephesians 6:11). Our struggle is not against flesh and blood, *"but against the rulers, against the powers, against the world forces of this darkness, against the spiritual forces of wickedness in the heavenly places"* (v.12).

Are you appropriately dressed for the battle? Are your loins girded with truth, and have you put on the breastplate of righteousness? (v.14) Are your feet shod with the Gospel of Peace? (v.15) Are you protected by the shield of faith? (v.16) Are you wearing the helmet of salvation and lifting the sword of the Spirit—which is the Word of God? (v.17) To be spiritually armed for the battle is the only way to resist the evil one. Finally, *"be strong in the Lord and in the strength of His might"* (Ephesians 6:10).

We are in a war—and we can't afford to surrender. When boxer James Corbett was the heavyweight champion of the world, he was asked, "What is the most important thing a man must do to become a champion?"

Corbett responded, "Be willing to fight one more round!"

HE'S DEFEATED!

Satan is still stalking the earth, but you can rejoice in the fact that he is a defeated foe waiting for his final punishment. As Paul writes: *"The God of peace will soon crush Satan under your feet"* (Romans 16:20).

In his great revelation, John saw an angel coming down from Heaven to take hold of Satan *"and he threw him into the abyss, and shut it and sealed it over him, so that he would not deceive the nations any longer"* (Revelation 20:3). The Bible assures us that the devil will be *"thrown into the lake of fire and...tormented day and night forever and ever"* (v.10).

We live in total victory because of the Blood of the Lamb and the word of our testimony (Revelation 12:11). That makes me shout "Hallelujah!"

"DELIVER US!"

Today, God gives us a choice. Will we serve the adversary or the Almighty? As Jesus declares: *"No one can serve two masters; for either he will hate the one and love the other, or he will be devoted to one and despise the other"* (Matthew 6:24).

The next time you pray the Lord's Prayer, mean it from the depths of your soul when you say, *"And do not lead us into temptation, but deliver us from evil"* (Matthew 6:13). You can defeat Satan and experience God's Kingdom, power and glory *forever!*

TEN STEPS TO MAKING WISE CHOICES

In making our decisions,
we must use the brains God has given us.
But we must also use our heart—
which He has also given us.

FULTON OURSLER

A 270-pound man in New York recently sued four fast food restaurants for jeopardizing his health with their greasy, fatty fare. He claimed they were at fault for his two heart attacks: "They never warned me about the dangers of certain ingredients," the man complained on a network news show.

Isn't it amazing how people can't seem to take responsibility for their own actions? Smokers become concerned when their health suddenly fails. Yet, on every pack of cigarettes the warning is clearly printed: "SURGEON GENERAL'S WARNING: Smoking Causes Lung Cancer, Heart Disease, Emphysema, And May Complicate Pregnancy."

This may be difficult for some people to comprehend, but *you* are in control of what goes into your body. Regardless of the consequences, your choices are your responsibility!

Who makes the choice for you to take drugs? Does someone force you to eat high-cholesterol foods? Is someone holding a gun to your head when you cheat on your spouse? Are you being coerced into maxing out your credit cards?

Your present circumstances are the direct result of your personal decisions—not the choices someone else has made for you. Remember, God has gifted you with the power to choose, and He holds you responsible for how you use this power.

THE RIGHT PATH

There's a fascinating account in the Old Testament of when God spoke to a young prophet from Judah and sent him on a mission. The Lord told him, "This is where I want you to go. This is what I want you to do and say. And when you are finished, come straight back—don't eat bread or drink water or return the same way you came."

So the young man obeyed the Lord, accomplished his mission, and was on his way home when he met an old man who was one of the prophets of God living in Bethel. He invited the young man to *"Come home with me and eat bread" (I Kings 13:15)*. At first, the traveler refused the invitation, but the old man continued: *"I also am a prophet like you, and an angel spoke to me by the word of the Lord, saying, 'Bring him back with you to your house, that he may eat bread and drink water.' But he lied to him" (v.18)*.

The young man of God from Judah allowed himself to be deceived and—instead of obeying God's instructions—chose to disobey. As a consequence of that unwise choice, he was devoured by a lion (v.26). God had clearly told the young prophet the right path to take. However, he listened to the voice of a stranger and met an untimely death.

Don't allow other people to tell you something different from what you know God has spoken to you. Stay true to what God has said. Obey Him. Don't allow yourself to be deceived by strangers with false claims that they pretend are from God—or from anyone else for that matter!

A SOUND STRATEGY

Today, the world has changed dramatically. We are bombarded with vast amounts of data, yet people continue repeatedly to make ill-advised choices. We have great knowledge, but not great wisdom. I believe there *is* a strategy for making sound, well-informed judgments day after day. Let me share theses ten important steps to help you make wise choices.

1. Pray.

The scientists or philosophers who believe they have all the answers to life are only fooling themselves. Their mental powers, no matter how far developed, are as a grain of sand compared with the Creator's omnipotence. *"With Him are wisdom and might; To Him belong counsel and understanding"* (Job 12:13).

It is not enough to rely solely on logic, reason or statistics. As Harry Truman once remarked, "How far would Moses have gone if he had taken a poll in Egypt?" We all desperately need the Lord's wisdom to guide us.

God knows you better than you know yourself. As the psalmist expresses: *"O Lord, You have searched me and known me. You know when I sit down and when I rise up; You understand my thought from afar. You scrutinize my path and my lying down, and are intimately acquainted with all my ways. Even before there is a word on my tongue; behold, O Lord, You know it all"* (Psalm 139:1-4).

Since God understands us so well, it only makes sense that we should ask for His direction in our lives. The Bible tells us: *"But if any of you lacks wisdom, let him ask of God, who gives to all generously and without reproach, and it will be given to him"* (James 1:5). That's why we must spend time with Him in prayer.

2. Read the Word.

The ultimate source of wise decision-making is as close as your Bible. The psalmist asks: *"How can a young man keep his way pure? By keeping it according to Your word"* (Psalm 119:9).

Why choose to stumble in the dark? Ask God to brighten your journey: *"The unfolding of Your words gives light; It gives understanding to the simple"* (v.130).

Yes, searching the Bible for direction is work, but it's

well worth the effort. Go to God's Word and "dig out" His truths!

Too many Christians expect somebody else, such as their pastor, to "spoon feed" Scripture to them. Don't expect someone else to do your work for you! Go to the Word yourself and discover what God is saying about the decisions you are facing.

The Word of God is filled with examples of choices people made—and the rewards and consequences they received as a result. Let their experience be your guide, and be certain your choices *always* line up with Scripture.

3. Sometimes, you need to fast.

Have you ever faced a challenge so monumental that you felt something in addition to prayer was needed? Something that would empower your prayers in the face of an overwhelming spiritual battle? The disciples experienced this when they prayed for a little boy who had a demon—yet nothing happened. When Jesus arrived on the scene, He immediately rebuked the demon and it *"came out of him, and the boy was cured at once" (Matthew 17:18).*

The disciples came to Jesus privately and asked, *"Why could we not drive it out?"* (v.19). Listen to the Lord's reply concerning casting out this stubborn demon: *"But this kind does not go out except by prayer and fasting" (Matthew 17:21).*

What are the toughest decisions you are facing? Remember: Major problems require extraordinary solutions! God wants to address the issue by giving you a fervent passion to pray and to fast. Sometimes its not enough to pray; sometimes its not enough to go to the Word; sometimes you need to fast. Fasting is a form of humbling yourself before God. When you humble yourself, God says He will exalt you. He'll give you the answer you need.

Jesus Himself told us to fast (Matthew 6:16-17). Fasting is a spiritual exercise that overcomes your flesh, allowing God to give you fresh revelation. When you fast, God moves obstacles that prayer alone will not remove.

4. Offer God a sacrifice.

When you are prayerfully seeking the answer you need, give the Lord an offering that costs you something. I'm not talking about the ceremonies of the Old Testament that involved animal blood sacrifices and rites of purification. Since Jesus became our sacrifice for sin on the Cross, these observances are no longer necessary.

The words "living sacrifice" may sound like a contradiction, yet that's what God asks us to become (Romans 12:1). Give to the Lord *every* part of you as your living sacrifice to Him:

- Your hands—so that your touch brings glory to the Lord.
- Your feet—to walk as Jesus would walk.
- Your eyes—to see as God sees.
- Your ears—to hear what the Lord is saying.
- Your tongue—to speak what is pleasing to the Father.
- Your mind—to make Godly choices.
- Your heart—to have a compassion and love for others.
- Your time, talents and treasure so that everything you are and have belongs to Him.

When you offer all that you are *completely* to the Lord, His decisions become yours.

5. Have a higher purpose.

If the options you are pursuing are purely for enhancing your image, building your reputation or boosting your ego, you'd better think twice, especially if your actions are motivated by envy, jealousy or revenge. God didn't place you on earth to be a superstar, or to "get even" with your enemies, but to have fellowship and communion with Him.

This is why before making a decision, you need to stop and ask yourself, "Will this choice bring honor and glory to the Lord?" As Paul wrote to the Believers at Colosse: *"Whatever you do in word or deed, do all in the name of the Lord Jesus, giving thanks through Him to God the Father" (Colossians 3:17).*

Never lose sight of the truth that God knows your every intention—and bases His rewards accordingly.

6. Weigh the alternatives.

Before blindly rushing ahead, ask yourself, "If I make this decision, what can I expect to take place?" Look at every possible scenario—the best that could happen AND the worst!

Look at the alternatives and think about the consequences:

- How will this decision affect those I love? *"He who troubles his own house will inherit the wind, And the foolish will be servant to the wisehearted" (Proverbs 11:29).*
- Will this decision strengthen my spiritual life? The end result should be *"for the equipping of the saints for the work of service, to the building up of the body of Christ" (Ephesians 4:12).*
- Is this decision in God's will? *"Commit your works to the Lord and your plans will be established" (Proverbs 16:3).*

The ultimate consequences of your choices may not be revealed until you stand before the Lord. The Apostle Paul prayed, *"that your love may abound still more and more in real knowledge and all discernment, so that you may approve the things that are excellent, in order to be sincere and blameless until the day of Christ"* (Philippians 1:9-10).

All of our choices need to be made with Eternity in view. Get those "scales" out. Weigh the alternatives carefully. What will be the consequence of making this choice or not making it? What are the alternatives?

7. Think your decisions through.

I'm sure you have been in the presence of someone whose mouth is in motion before his mind is in gear—speaking before thinking! King Solomon had an opinion about such a man: *"He who gives an answer before he hears; it is folly and shame to him"* (Proverbs 18:13).

In the world of carpentry, there's a rule that says "measure twice and cut once." That is sound advice. Instead of rushing into a hasty plan, take time to carefully weigh the advantages and disadvantages.

Follow the example of the lowly ants, and do some advance preparation. These small creatures decide in August what they'll be eating in January. *"Go to the ant, O sluggard, observe her ways and be wise, which, having no chief, officer or ruler, prepares her food in the summer and gathers her provision in the harvest"* (Proverbs 6:6-8).

You may wonder, "How can I plan ahead when I may need to make a lightning-fast judgment in a crisis? What if there is no time for analyzing the situation?" Believe me when I tell you that reading and memorizing Scripture will give you the necessary tools to make instant choices. You will know how to fight the attacks of Satan, claim God's healing power and connect with Heaven. In the words of the psalmist, *"Your word I have treasured in my heart, that I may not sin against You"* (Psalm 119:11). Also remember: *"Wise men store up knowledge, but with the mouth of the foolish, ruin is at hand"* (Proverbs 10:14).

Every time I am hit with a crisis—whether traveling in an airplane with a failed engine or facing a health emergency—out of my mouth begins to flow Scripture after Scripture. Often, I don't even remember having memorized the verses, yet I can quote them by heart. Backed by the Word and God's Promises, I feel comfortable about making the necessary immediate decisions.

8. Seek Godly counsel.

I know it's human nature to think, "Look, I can do it by myself," yet you always need God's guidance and advice. Seeking help doesn't mean you are weak. In reality, it is a sign of strength!

In addition to finding direction, the Lord desires that we are spiritually accountable. If the great leaders of the Bible sought wisdom and help, why shouldn't you? Moses had his father-in-law, Jethro, while Paul turned to Barnabas and the elders of the church. Read the book of Proverbs and you'll understand what I mean. It has much to say concerning the need to seek Godly counsel:

- *"He who walks with wise men will be wise, but the companion of fools will suffer harm"* (Proverbs 13:20).
- *"For by wise guidance you will wage war, and in abundance of counselors there is victory"* (Proverbs 24:6).
- *"Listen to counsel and accept discipline, that you may be wise the rest of your days"* (Proverbs 19:20).
- *"Without consultation, plans are frustrated, but with many counselors they succeed"* (Proverbs 15:22).

Don't blindly accept every offer of advice at face value, or you may wind up receiving counsel from the devil himself. Be on the alert for wolves in sheep's clothing. Speaking with His disciples on the Mount of Olives, Jesus warned: *"If anyone says to you, 'Behold, here is the*

Christ,' or 'There He is,' do not believe him. For false Christs and false prophets will arise and will show great signs and wonders, so as to mislead, if possible, even the elect" (Matthew 24:23-24).

There's no need to announce your problems to the world. Be discrete. This is why you need to choose a trusted counselor who will keep what you say in total confidence.

Before you allow someone to speak into your life, know the background of the individual. Find a Believer who is grounded in the Word and lives a blameless life. Specifically, look for a person who has experienced what you are now facing. It's always encouraging to listen to someone who has "been there" and, with God's help, has emerged victorious.

Remember, Godly counsel—if it's truly from God—is going to confirm something that God's already spoken to you. Godly counsel always lines up with the Word of God. He *never* goes against His Word.

After being married for over 30 years, I've learned that before making a major decision, I talk the situation over with Barbara. Her input on the issue is more than vital— it's Scriptural. The Lord asks: *"Can two walk together, except they be agreed?"* (Amos 3:3 KJV).

Perhaps the Lord has given you a vision for the future, and you need to talk with someone who has already reached a similar goal. The advice you receive may allow you to avoid dangerous pitfalls. However, let me offer this word of caution to you: never rely on man more than you rely on God. If the Lord has revealed something to you directly—either through His clear voice or through the Word—act on that Divine directive first. After all, *"There is no wisdom and no understanding, and no counsel against* the Lord" (Proverbs 21:30). When you believe you've already heard from God, the counselor's role is to confirm what the Lord has told you.

9. Be led by peace.

People have asked: "David, how do you truly know you've made the right decision?" I love to answer, "Because I have a peace about it!" To me, that's how the Lord confirms His will and His Word.

When peace rules, the Lord becomes like an umpire, resolving issues and letting you know what is right. I love the words of Paul as written in the Amplified Bible: *"And let the peace from Christ rule (act as an umpire continually) in your hearts [deciding and settling with finality all questions that arise in your minds, in that peaceful state] to which as [members of Christ's] one body you were called [to live]"* (Colossians 3:15).

Also, when you make a decision contrary to God's will, you will know it. There will be a restlessness—an uneasy feeling in the pit of your stomach. That's the Lord telling you to put things on hold, perhaps even to back up and to reverse the choice you have made. I've observed those who make choices out of disobedience or rebellion. They balk and insist, "I'm not going to do that." But when a decision is made out of a pure heart and a desire to please the Lord, I believe He will honor you.

If your decision is the wrong one but has been made out of the integrity of your heart, you can go to God and say, "Lord, I took this step because I believed it was what You wanted me to do. Now I'm asking You to help me in this situation—to lead me to the place You need me to be." Before long, the Lord will open new doors or perhaps bring someone or something into your life to steer you back to the right path.

When in doubt, go back to peace. Return to the moment when you first felt God speak to you. What was it that caused your heart to feel His comfort and assurance? Make a U-turn and recapture that peace before you proceed any further.

Pray that *"the peace of God, which surpasses all comprehension, will guard your hearts and your minds in Christ Jesus"* (Philippians 4:7).

Don't move in one direction or another, don't make a choice until you get peace in your spirit. Don't move. Don't move forward. Don't move backwards. Don't move to the left. Don't move to the right. Don't move, *period,* until God gives you peace in your spirit.

10. Stay committed to your decision.

Once you make a choice, be determined to see it through unless and until God gives you some other specific direction. The world will encourage you to have a backup strategy—just in case your first plan doesn't work. With God's guidance in your life, there is no need for a "Plan B."

When you know what the Lord has specifically told you but it hasn't come to pass, examine your steps to see if you took a wrong turn somewhere. Never blame God. Instead, ask His forgiveness if you weren't persistent and faithful to His plan.

Accept what the Lord tells you and don't be tempted to vacillate. The Bible cautions: *"For he that wavereth is like a wave of the sea driven with the wind and tossed. For let not that man think that he shall receive any thing of the Lord. A double minded man is unstable in all his ways"* (James 1:6-8 KJV).

Everyone goes through tough times, and you will be challenged regarding your choices. Expect it! Jesus says:

"In the world ye shall have tribulation: but be of good cheer; I have overcome the world" (John 16:33 KJV).

If the Lord Jesus has emerged victorious, then as His child—so will you!

SHE WOULDN'T LEAVE

There's power in persistence! Become like the woman who came to Elisha when her son was dying. When she reached the man of God, she grabbed his feet and wouldn't let go! The prophet tried to have his servant, Gehazi, go to the dying boy and lay Elisha's wooden staff on the child's face. Still, the woman insisted, boldly announcing: *"As the Lord lives and as you yourself live, I will not leave you" (II Kings 4:30).*

The prophet walked with the woman to her house and saw the boy lying dead on his couch. Elisha went in to him, shut the door, and began calling on God. The Bible records that *"he went up and lay on the child, and put his mouth on his mouth and his eyes on his eyes and his hands on his hands, and he stretched himself on him; and the flesh of the child became warm" (II Kings 4:34).* Suddenly, the boy sneezed seven times and opened his eyes. He was completely healed! The mother's persistence led to a miracle!

DON'T LOSE HEART!

Jesus tells the story of a judge who cared little about the people he served. In

that same town lived a widow who kept coming to him with the same plea: *"Grant me justice against my adversary" (Luke 18:3).*

For quite a while, the judge couldn't be bothered and refused to help her. But finally, he said to himself, *"Even though I do not fear God nor respect man, yet because this widow bothers me, I will give her legal protection, otherwise by continually coming she will wear me out." (vv.4-5).*

Why did Jesus share this parable with His disciples? It was to tell them to be as persistent as the widow and *"that at all times they ought to pray and not to lose heart" (v.1).*

When you have followed God's principles for making wise choices, step out in faith and be decisive. You'll be amazed at what takes place when you choose to walk in God's assurance and act on His authority.

11

DETERMINE YOUR ETERNAL DESTINY

When ten thousand, times
ten thousand, times
ten thousand years have passed,
eternity will have just begun.

BILLY SUNDAY

I once heard about a gardener working for a large estate in northern Italy who was giving a visitor a tour of the beautifully manicured grounds. Just before the tourist left he said, "Let me commend you for the fantastic way you keep up the property. It's perfect!" Then he asked, "By the way, when was the last time the owner was here?"

The gardener paused for a moment and replied, "It was about ten years ago."

Surprised at the answer, the visitor asked, "Then why do you keep these gardens in such immaculate condition?"

"Because I'm expecting him to return," responded the groundskeeper.

The visitor continued, "Is he coming next week?"

The gardener shrugged his shoulders and answered, "I don't know exactly when he is coming, but it could be today." Instead of looking down the road impatiently waiting for his master's return, the gardener was busy at his work, trimming the hedges and planting flowers.

THE GREAT SEPARATION!

My friend, we are about to experience the soon return of *our* Master—and the day is closer than we can imagine. The Lord declares: *"Behold, I am coming quickly, and My reward is with Me, to render to every man according to what he has done" (Revelation 22:12).*

You may respond, "Wait a minute! That sounds as though the 'reward' could be amazing or awful, depending on how we live on earth." This is exactly true.

In His parable concerning the sheep and the goats, Jesus explains what is going to occur. He says, *"But when the Son of Man comes in His glory, and all the angels with Him, then He will sit on His glorious throne. All the nations will be gathered before Him; and He will separate them from one another, as the shepherd separates the sheep from the goats"* (Matthew 25:31-32).

Jesus continues, *"and He will put the sheep on His right, and the goats on the left. Then the King will say to those on His right, 'Come, you who are blessed of My Father, inherit the kingdom prepared for you from the foundation of the world'"* (vv.33-34).

Eternal existence is waiting for *every* person. *"These* [speaking of those who did not serve the Lord] *will go away into eternal punishment, but the righteous into eternal life"* (v.46).

YOU WILL BE REPAID

When Jesus was invited to eat at the home of a prominent man, He asked His host to give a banquet and invite the poor, the crippled, the lame and the blind, *"and you will be blessed, since they do not have the means to repay you; for you will be repaid at the resurrection of the righteous"* (Luke 14:14).

The word Jesus used for "repaid" is *apodidomai*—*apo* meaning "back" and *didomai* meaning "to give." The Lord was telling the man, "For what you give, you will be given back." It's the same word Jesus used in telling the story of the Good Samaritan: *"When I return I will repay you"* (Luke 10:35). And Jesus tells us, *"For whoever gives you a cup of water to drink because of your name as followers of Christ, truly I say to you, he will not lose his reward"* (Mark 9:41).

Payday is coming! One day soon, we *all* will stand in the Presence of God, and He will reward us for the choices we have made and the actions we have taken here on earth.

WHAT ABOUT DEEDS?

Let me remind you again that your choices not only determine *where* you will spend eternity, but *how*.

Many Believers aren't concerned about what awaits them "on the other side"—their primary concern is knowing that they are *going* to Heaven. They'll be surprised when they stand before God and realize their rewards are not based simply on salvation. Remember, Jesus has already paid that price for you, and your faith in Him gains you entry into Heaven. Once there, you will be judged based on what you did as a Believer: your works and the Seeds you have Sown. Yes, every man will be repaid *"according to his deeds" (Matthew 16:27)*.

To put it as simply as I know how, your eternal destination is based on your belief—and your actions based on your beliefs. For example, God's Word says, *"If you confess* [action] *with your mouth Jesus as Lord, and believe* [belief] *in your heart that God raised Him from the dead, you will be saved; for with the heart a person believes, resulting in righteousness, and with the mouth he confesses, resulting in salvation" (Romans 10:9-10)*.

The consequences of this decision will determine *where* you will spend your everlasting future. The other choices we make in life—including our behavior— unlock the door to Heaven's rewards and determine *how* we will spend eternity. Your actions in this life have a direct bearing on what Heaven will be like for you.

THE SECRET OF ABUNDANCE

The Almighty is also going to judge us based on the spiritual light we possess (Luke 12:48). He will ask us,

"What was the motivation of your heart? What did you do with your talents and abilities?"

Jesus told the story of a man who was going on a journey. Before leaving, he called his servants and entrusted his property to them—giving each one different amounts of talents (money). The servant who received five talents put the money to work and gained five more. The one with two talents gained two more. But the man who received just one talent dug a hole in the ground and hid his master's money.

After a long time, the owner returned home. When he learned what the first two servants had accomplished, he exclaimed, *"Well done, good and faithful slave. You were faithful with a few things, I will put you in charge of many things; enter into the joy of your master"* (Matthew 25:23).

The servant who was afraid and hid his talent was admonished: *"You wicked, lazy slave...you ought to have put my money in the bank, and on my arrival I would have received my money back with interest"* (Matthew 25:27). Then he took the hidden talent and gave it to the servant who already had *ten* talents.

Through this parable, Jesus teaches this important lesson: *"For to everyone who has, more shall be given, and he will have an abundance; but from the one who does not have, even what he does have shall be taken away. Throw out the worthless slave into the outer darkness; in that place there will be weeping and gnashing of teeth"* (vv.29-30).

THE ULTIMATE REWARD

I hope you realize how close we are to the Second Coming of Christ. The Bible tells us what is about to take place: *"For the Lord Himself will descend from heaven with a shout, with the voice of the archangel and with the trumpet of God, and the dead in Christ will rise first, then we who are alive and remain will be caught up together with them in the clouds to meet the Lord in the air, and so we shall always be with the Lord" (I Thessalonians 4:16-17).*

Even as I write these words, God is putting the finishing touches on your reward. Jesus says, *"If I go and prepare a place for you, I will come again and receive you to Myself, that where I am, there you may be also" (John 14:3).*

WHAT A PLACE!

Heaven—mentioned 632 times in the Bible—is going to be a reward beyond anything our earthly minds can imagine. I remember hearing about a little girl who was taking an evening walk with her father. She looked up at the stars and exclaimed, "Oh, Daddy, if the wrong side of Heaven is so beautiful, what must the right side be like!"

The Bible tells us "Eye hath not seen, nor ear heard, neither have entered into the heart of man, the things which God hath prepared for them that love him" (I Corinthians 2:9).

What a place Heaven will be! Every tear will be wiped from our eyes *"and there will no longer be any death; there will no longer be any mourning, or crying, or pain; the first things have passed away" (Revelation 21:4).*

Just think what you're about to experience! You will…
…eat of the tree of life (Revelation 2:7).
…receive hidden manna (v.17).
…be arrayed in white garments (Revelation 3:5).
…have your name written in the Book of Life (v.5).
…have your name confessed by Christ before the
   Father (v.5).

...be a pillar in the Temple of God (v.12).
...sit with Christ on His throne (v.21).

WHAT—AND WHERE—ARE YOU SOWING?

Specifically, what are you choosing to do today that will prepare you for God's great tomorrow? When you invest in something bigger than yourself, you will receive a greater reward. That's why I encourage you to Sow into Good Ground. In Matthew 13 the Bible describes different levels of Harvests—some thirty—some sixty—some one hundred fold. It's sad to say, but not every church or ministry is good ground. Some churches and ministries will yield only a thirty or sixty fold increase. I encourage you to invest your Seed where it will bring the greatest return for the Kingdom of God.

BLESSING AND CURSING—LIFE OR DEATH—CHOICES AND REWARDS.

I want to deposit three Scriptures into your spirit as we close.

One, Deuteronomy 11:26-28: *"Behold, I set before you this day a choice, a blessing and a curse. A blessing if you obey the commandments of the Lord, your God, which I command you this day and a curse if you will not obey the commandments of the Lord but turn aside out of the way that I have commanded you this day."*

Two, Jeremiah 21:8: *"And unto this people, thou shall say, "Thus saith the Lord. Behold, I set before you the way of life, and the way of death" (KJV).*

Three, Deuteronomy 30:19 and 20: *"I call heaven and earth to record this day against you, that I have set before you life and death, blessing and cursing: therefore choose life, that both you and your seed may live: That you would love the Lord your God, and that you would obey his voice, and that you would cleave unto him: for he is your life, and the length of your days."*

In the Introduction of this book, I shared how the Lord was impressing upon me that there were three kinds of people who needed the message contained within these pages. I don't know what kind of choices you're facing today or what category of people you're in. You may be one who is about to make a terrible choice that you're going to regret forever. You may be one who is about to make one of the greatest choices you'll ever imagine. You may be one who is sitting in the land of indecision.

I challenge you today to choose wisely—choose *LIFE*—choose obedience. If you want to change your future, you must change your choices. Your future is shaped by the choices you make in this life, and the rewards you will receive in Heaven are going to be based on the *deposits* you made *there* from the *choices* you made *here.* Choose wisely.

Barbara and I want to pray with you and for you today. We want to agree in prayer with you that God will help you make the right choices, choices that will bring great rewards now in this lifetime AND in the world to come.

Let's pray together right now:

Father, we come together before you in the name of Jesus. Thank You for Your Word and that You have set before us life and death, blessings and curses. Thank You that You desire for us to choose wisely so that You can reward us with Your good gifts.

Speak to us through Your Word in our times of prayer. Speak to us through Godly counsel.

May we hear Your voice clearly as we humble ourselves through fasting before You. Speak clearly to us and help us to know, "This is the way, walk ye in it!"

Father, for those who are on the brink of making a critically wrong choice at this moment, whoever they are, wherever they might be, we pray in Jesus' Name that they will stop. Help them, Lord, to look to You for Your help and the wisdom to make the right decision. As difficult as it may be for them to obey You, give them the strength to choose wisely.

Lord, for those who are on the verge of making some of the greatest choices they'll ever make in their life, let Your rewards be theirs, in this life and in the world to come.

Father, help all of our choices to be like gold, silver and precious stones. Don't let our choices be those that will burn up as hay, wood and stubble. Help us not to suffer loss by making wrong choices.

Lord, for those who are in the valley of indecision and doubt, I pray You will move them by the power of Your Holy Spirit to make right, wise, and obedient choices. Take away their fear and give them faith. Replace their doubt and despair with courage and hope.

Help us, Father, to choose wisely how we Sow our time, our talent and our treasure, since Your rewards for obedience are beyond measure. Help us to choose wisely. In Jesus' Name. Amen.

WE ARE HERE FOR YOU!

My friend, I want to assure you that God has a marvelous plan for your life—and He offers you right choices that He is asking you to make. This is why I encourage you to trust in the Lord with all your heart and let Him direct your path.

As you face these vital decisions, please know Barbara and I are praying that you will make your decisions according to the Father's will—choices that will fulfill His purpose for you.

During those troublesome times when you feel you've taken a wrong path, simply stop and say: "Lord, I'm sorry. I am asking you to bring me back to the place I need to be. Lead me into your perfect plan."

We are praying with you, rejoicing with you, and believing together that the choices you make will bring God's great rewards—that His best will be performed in your life, now, and in the life to come.

Remember, *We Are Here for You!*

A SCRIPTURAL GUIDE TO CHOICES AND REWARDS

Life is a series of daily decisions. We constantly ask ourselves, "Should I open this door or leave it closed? Should I take the path to the right or travel the road that goes left?"

In this book, we examined how choices affect our relationships, our reputation, our riches and our righteousness. However, the most important question we should ask is, "What does God say about my choices?"

I encourage you to open your Bible and discover what happens as the result of your decisions. Take the time to read these Scriptures in their context and apply them to your life:

YOUR CHOICE:

When you choose to believe on Christ as your Savior—

YOUR REWARD:

You will spend eternity with Him (I John 5:13).

or

YOUR CHOICE:

When you choose to be stubborn and unrepentant—

YOUR REWARD:

You are storing up wrath for yourself and God's judgment (Romans 2:5).

YOUR CHOICE:

When you choose to Sow bountifully—

YOUR REWARD:

You will Reap bountifully (II Corinthians 9:6).

or

YOUR CHOICE:

When you choose to Sow sparingly—

YOUR REWARD:

You will Reap sparingly (II Corinthians 9:6).

YOUR CHOICE:

When you choose to repent and ask God's forgiveness—

YOUR REWARD:

He will hear and answer you (Isaiah 1:15-16).

or

YOUR CHOICE:

When you choose to live in sin—

YOUR REWARD:

Your prayers are not answered and poverty comes (I Kings 8:33-35).

YOUR CHOICE:

When you choose to spend time in God's Presence—

YOUR REWARD:

He will bless you with peace and abundance (I Chronicles 13:14).

or

YOUR CHOICE:

When you place your faith in others instead of the Lord—

YOUR REWARD:

You will receive His judgment (II Kings 1:3-4).

YOUR CHOICE:

When you choose to Sow good Seed into your children—

YOUR REWARD:

They will receive a lifetime of blessing (I Chronicles 22:12-13).

or

YOUR CHOICE:

When you choose to live in disobedience –

YOUR REWARD:

It can affect your descendants forever (II Kings 5:27).

YOUR CHOICE:

When you choose to return to the Lord –

YOUR REWARD:

You will find compassion, grace and forgiveness (II Chronicles 30:9).

or

YOUR CHOICE:

When you choose to become friends with the wicked –

YOUR REWARD:

God's wrath will fall upon you (II Chronicles 19:2).

YOUR CHOICE:

When you choose to humble yourself before the Lord –

YOUR REWARD:

He will hear your prayer (II Chronicles 34:27).

or

YOUR CHOICE

When you choose to be proud –

YOUR REWARD

God will resist you (I Peter 4:6).

YOUR CHOICE:

When you choose to love the Lord –

YOUR REWARD:

*He will deliver you and set you on high
(Psalm 91: 14).*

or

YOUR CHOICE:

*When you choose to make an alliance that is not of
God –*

YOUR REWARD:

*You will receive shame and humiliation
(Isaiah 30:1-3).*

YOUR CHOICE:

*When you choose to acquire God's wisdom and
understanding –*

YOUR REWARD:

He will exalt you (Proverbs 4:7).

or

YOUR CHOICE:

*When you choose to neglect God's counsel and refuse
His correction –*

YOUR REWARD:

*You will eat the fruit of your own ways.
(Proverbs 1:24-26).*

YOUR CHOICE:

*When you choose to trust in the Lord with all your
heart and acknowledge Him in all your ways –*

YOUR REWARD:

He will make your paths straight (Proverbs 3:5-6).

or

YOUR CHOICE:

When you choose to walk according to the stubbornness of your own heart –

YOUR REWARD:

The Lord will declare calamity against you (Jeremiah 16:10-12).

YOUR CHOICE:

When you choose to honor the Lord with the first and best of what you have –

YOUR REWARD:

You will always have plenty (Proverbs 3:9).

or

YOUR CHOICE:

When you choose to give the Lord your second best –

YOUR REWARD:

He is not pleased and does not accept your offering (Malachi 1:6-10).

YOUR CHOICE:

When you choose to give attention to the Lord and refuse to be enticed with the things of this world –

YOUR REWARD:

All your ways will be established (Proverbs 4:20-27).

or

YOUR CHOICE:

When you choose to gain the whole world and forfeit your soul –

YOUR REWARD:

It will profit you nothing (Matthew 16:26).

YOUR CHOICE:

When you choose to place your hope and trust in the Lord –

YOUR REWARD:

You will become as a tree planted by the water (Jeremiah 7:7-8).

or

YOUR CHOICE:

When you choose to turn from God and trust in your own strength –

YOUR REWARD:

You will inhabit the wilderness (Jeremiah 17:5-6).

YOUR CHOICE:

When you choose to Sow your tithes and offerings into the storehouse of God –

YOUR REWARD:

He will open the windows of heaven and pour out a blessing you cannot contain (Malachi 3:10).

or

YOUR CHOICE:

When you choose to rob God with your tithes and offerings –

YOUR REWARD:

You are cursed with a curse (Malachi 3:8-9).

The Creator couldn't have made it any more clear. For every decision you make, there is a consequence and for every choice, there is a reward.

What God declared to the children of Israel, He is also saying to you: *"I call heaven and earth to witness against* you today, that I have set before you life and death, the blessing and the curse. So choose life in order that you may live, you and your descendants, by loving the Lord your God, by obeying His voice, and by holding fast to Him; for this is your life and the length of your days" (Deuteronomy 30:19-20).

THE CHOICE IS *YOURS!*

ABOUT THE AUTHOR

DAVID CERULLO is a unique combination of Christian minister and corporate businessman. The son of international evangelist Morris Cerullo, David took a less traditional approach to ministry, graduating from Oral Roberts University with a degree in Business Administration and Management.

After college, David put that degree to work when he joined Morris Cerullo World Evangelism and gradually assumed most of the responsibility for the day-to-day operations. He was ordained in 1974, and while in ministry with his dad and working on various personal projects of his own, David acquired skills and experience in construction project management and real estate development that ran the spectrum from major hotels and commercial office buildings to single family dwellings.

David also worked extensively throughout Europe, Latin American, Africa, and Asia organizing numerous international projects for both ministry and business. He founded a successful advertising and public relations firm, a construction company, and a management-consulting firm.

Because David has a passion to impact lives for Christ worldwide through the media, in 1990 he combined his strong business skills with his passion for ministry to assume the leadership of Inspirational Network, a fledgling cable television network. With God's help and guidance, David has built the cable channel into a far-reaching media ministry. Today, THE INSPIRATION NETWORKS include INSP, a Christian cable network offering more than 70 different ministries across the country; iLife-TV, America's first digital Christian network; and La Familia, a Spanish-language network for Hispanic families coast to coast. This ministry of The Inspiration Networks is now reaching into 26 million households nationwide.

David is a member of the National Cable Television Association, the Cable and Telecommunications Association for Marketing, and the National Association of Television Program Executives. He serves on the Board of Directors for the National Religious Broadcasters Association, The Inspiration Networks, and Morris Cerullo World Evangelism.

David and his wife Barbara have been married for more than 30 years and have two adult children and three grandchildren. Together, David and Barbara Cerullo host the daily national television series "Inspiration Today!"

THE INSPIRATION NETWORKS PRODUCT RESOURCES BRINGING YOU INSPIRATION, ENCOURAGEMENT, AND HOPE!

God's Answers for Anxious Times

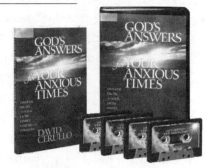

God plans no defeats for your life, but the devil does! *God's Answers for Your Anxious Times* is a book with four audio-cassettes filled with God's wisdom and encouragement for your circumstances. Learn how to deal with the anxious times in your life with these anointed, hope-filled messages that will bring you God's Presence, Comfort, and Peace whenever you are fearful, overwhelmed, or anxious.

For your Seed gift of $20 or more (00171BCR)

"Inspiration Today!" Devotional Magazine

Through this monthly publication, Believers across the country have experienced the power of God's Word and been blessed by stories of encouragement to help them grow in their faith. Filled with daily devotionals, testimonies, and personal messages from David and Barbara Cerullo, you'll discover this magazine to be a great resource as you daily walk in the power of the Holy Spirit and the authority of God's Word.

For your Seed gift of $25 or more (ITMBCR)

Turn Off the Darkness / Cassettes

With more than 30 years of media experience, David Cerullo offers you a wealth of spiritual insight and practical wisdom to help you redeem your family's television viewing experience and protect your home from its harmful influences. This book-on-tape is a timely treatment for Believers who desire to raise a righteous standard and allow God to use them to change their world.

For your Seed gift of $20.00 or more (00181BCR)

The Price of Freedom / VHS Video

Receive encouragement and strength from the testimonies of others who have faced disasters, personal crisis, and torture, yet have come forth victorious because of God's faithfulness. Filmed from our nation's capitol in Washington, D.C., these testimonies of the Lord's protection and strength will empower your walk with Him. This video also makes an excellent Evangelism tool for sharing with the unsaved!

For your Seed gift of $25.00 or more (00169BCR)

When you order ministry products from us, you will be blessed by these excellent message, *AND* you will be Sowing Seed for Souls! Your Seed gift Sown into the Good Ground of The Inspiration Networks Reaps an Uncommon Harvest for God's Kingdom *AND* for your eternity in Heaven as we minister together to the Lost and strengthen the Body of Christ across America.

To order our Ministry Resources, please visit our website at **www.insptoday.com** You may also write to us at:

> David Cerullo
> The Inspiration Networks
> P.O. Box 7750
> Charlotte, NC 28241-7750.

Monday—Friday at 10:00 p.m. (EST)
**Bringing you God's
Encouragement, Inspiration, and Hope!**